SPEAKING
FOR GOD

WITNESS LEE

Living Stream Ministry
Anaheim, California

First Edition, November 2001.

ISBN 0-7363-1463-6

Published by

Living Stream Ministry
2431 W. La Palma Ave., Anaheim, CA 92801 U.S.A.
P. O. Box 2121, Anaheim, CA 92814 U.S.A.

Printed in the United States of America

01 02 03 04 05 06 07 / 10 9 8 7 6 5 4 3 2 1

CONTENTS

PREFACE

This book is a translation of messages given in Chinese by Brother Witness Lee on November 11-14, 1985 in Singapore. These messages were not reviewed by the speaker.

CHAPTER ONE

THE PRESENT SITUATION
AND THE FUTURE OUTLOOK

THE PRESENT SITUATION OF THE CHURCHES
IN THE LORD'S RECOVERY

In the spring of 1949, the Lord's recovery took a step forward when some saints moved from mainland China to Taiwan. In recent days we have gathered some statistics on all the churches on the earth today. From this "official" survey, we have obtained accurate information showing that on this earth there are presently more than six hundred churches in the Lord's recovery spread over five continents. We have not included mainland China in the statistics because we are not clear about its true situation.

In 1949 there were approximately eighty to ninety churches outside of mainland China, most of them being in Southeast Asia. At that time there were no churches in either Japan or Korea, and in Taiwan there were only five or six very small churches. For example, the church in Taipei had no more than a few dozen saints meeting in a Japanese-style house made of straw mats. In Hong Kong there was only one locality with a church. In Southeast Asia the churches were concentrated mostly in four countries: Indonesia, Thailand, Malaysia, and the Philippines. Further south toward Burma and India, there was some contact with a small number of people but no formal meetings anywhere. Therefore, the total estimate was at the most eighty to ninety churches.

After we were sent to start the work in Taiwan, the Lord was able to gain scores of churches on the island of Taiwan. During this time the publications we put out were used by the Lord in many ways. For example, the first publication we began upon our arrival in Taiwan was a magazine called *The Ministry of the Word,* which included a special series of issues entitled *A Supplement on Fundamental Truths.* Later this special series on the truth was published in a volume called *Fundamental Truths in the Scriptures.* The Lord greatly blessed this publication in the Philippines, particularly in the southern part. Within a period of ten to fifteen years the Lord raised up almost one hundred churches on the island of Mindanao alone through the *Fundamental Truths in the Scriptures.*

In 1958 the Lord led us to spread to the Western world; in particular we were led to contact America. Due to this contact we received the burden to spread the work of the Lord's recovery to America. By the end of 1962 we were very clear that we should take up this burden. Moreover, we were clear that we should not direct our work only toward the Chinese community in America, as most of the Chinese evangelists or pastors had done. Amazingly, our work reached the Caucasian Americans from the very onset. Thus, the work of the Lord's recovery entered into the English-speaking Western world from the very beginning.

By the year 1960 the number of churches had increased from a base number of eighty to ninety in 1949 to a total of approximately two hundred fifty. This included an increase of fifty to sixty churches in Taiwan, about one hundred churches in the southern part of the Philippines, and two to three churches in Japan. Thus, before the Lord's recovery spread to the Western world, there were already two hundred fifty churches in the Far East.

A total of twenty-three years has passed since the inception of the work of the Lord's recovery in America in 1962 to today. During this time, because the Lord's work has been predominantly in the English-speaking world, it has spread from America to the other continents—to Europe, Australia, Africa, and also to Central and South America. This expansion has not been very fast or widespread, but during these twenty-three years, the Lord's recovery has established at least three hundred seventy churches in the Western world.

Adding these to the ones in the Far East, we have a total of about six hundred twenty to six hundred fifty local churches.

The point I am making here is that, on the one hand, we dare not say that this expansion has been very fast or very widespread, yet on the other hand, we must bow our heads in worship to the Lord because He has truly been working among us. On the five continents there are about forty countries with churches in the Lord's recovery. In addition, this number does not include mainland China. This is a matter we all must see.

INTERNAL PROBLEMS AND EXTERNAL TROUBLES IN THE ADVANCE OF THE LORD'S RECOVERY

While we have been greatly blessed by the Lord during these twenty-three years, nevertheless, we have also experienced many twists and turns, especially in America. On the one hand, there has been the Lord's blessing, yet on the other hand, there has been the enemy's attack. During these twenty-three years there have been both internal problems and external troubles. The internal problems were due to the fact that some of those who had been brought into the Lord's recovery had ulterior motives. The initiation of the Lord's recovery in America was brand new and full of vitality, and it was particularly substantial and living in its content—the truth. When the Lord's recovery came to America, its most pronounced and striking characteristic was its richness in the truth. In the second year after we started the work of the Lord's recovery, we began to put out publications. By 1985 we had put out over three thousand messages with a total of about thirty to forty thousand pages. This has been the general situation.

Furthermore, we all know that in America there are many large Christian denominations. For example, the Southern Baptist Church, a very large denomination, has about eleven to thirteen million members. There are also several others with a few million members. They are all very large organizations. Compared to them, we are less than a tenth of one percent. Nevertheless, though we are a very small group, we may be ahead as far as the number of publications is concerned. As a result, two kinds of people have constantly paid attention to us. One kind feels that the recovery is something brand new with a great future, so they come in thinking that they can gain something here, hoping that some day they can "take over" the Lord's recovery. This is the internal problem.

The external troubles came from some people in a certain Christian group who wrote books to oppose us. They had planned to publish a book to oppose Brother Watchman Nee. However, right after 1975 when they were about to publish their book, they felt after much consideration that since Brother Nee's books were having tremendous impact in America and Europe at that time that it would not be easy to put down Brother Nee. Hence, they decided to put me down first before they attacked Brother Nee.

The few opposing books that they published caused us considerable harm. Two of the books were "deadly poison" in that they compared us to a certain evil group, depicting us as being even worse than those people, whose evil deeds were publicized throughout the world at that time. As a result, the American brothers and sisters among us, especially the young people, were the first ones to suffer much persecution. Many of their parents read these books and became alarmed. In many cases, if their children were active in the churches, the parents concluded that their children had been wrongly influenced, and they immediately took certain actions that brought considerable suffering to these young saints.

The path taken by the Lord's recovery has always been a persecuted and narrow way. We do not expect to be embraced by the worldly people. However, after the publication of the second editions of those two evil books at the end of 1979, we nearly had no way to carry out our work any longer. The reason was that once people came into contact with those two evil books, they were finished, no matter which campus in America they attended and no matter whether they were new believers, unbelievers, or even believers of many years. Everyone who read those books believed that they were true.

In 1980 the co-workers came together and felt that as long as those two books existed, our work could no longer be carried out; we had come to an impasse. When the second book, *The God-Men*, arrived in England, the "poison" in that book damaged many localities there. In previous years there had been churches in over eight places, but in the past two to three years it has become impossible to bring anyone into the church. In America the greatest pain has come from the parents of the young saints. Once affected by the poison, the parents would spend a great deal of money to hire certain persons to "counsel" their children. They used every means, at times even exhausting their financial reserves, in the belief that they were rescuing their children. In Germany the situation was even more serious; many saints in schools, hospitals, and government agencies lost their jobs, and when they tried to find new employment, they were rejected. This is the external trouble in which we have been persecuted to such a degree.

A LAWSUIT CONTENDING FOR THE TRUTH

As a result, after much consideration, we felt that we had to imitate Paul. In 1 Corinthians 6 Paul said that it is wrong for brother to go to court with brother, especially before unbelievers (v. 6). However, in Acts 20 and 21 we see a different situation. Paul had originally intended to sail directly to Jerusalem from Greece, but due to a plot made against him by the Jews, he resolved to change direction. Instead of returning directly to Jerusalem from Greece, he turned toward the north to Macedonia, and then passing through Macedonia he returned to Jerusalem. This was Paul's wisdom through which he escaped the pursuit and ambush set by the Jews (20:1-3).

When Paul entered Jerusalem, however, those in Jerusalem who had compromised with Judaism, including James, the leading elder, persuaded him to take several men who had a vow on themselves to be purified with them. Paul went along with them and did accordingly. Toward the end of the seven days of purification, the Jews from Asia who had been in pursuit of Paul came to Jerusalem, and seeing him in the temple they began to shout and cry out, laying their hands on him. At that very time the news came to the commander of the cohort. The commander was a chiliarch in the Roman military who was in command of a thousand troops for the purpose of maintaining peace. In other words, he was the chief of the garrison in Jerusalem. When he heard the report, he felt that it was his responsibility to handle the situation and not allow the uproar to continue lest the matter get worse. Hence, he quickly brought soldiers and centurions to rescue Paul out of the hands of the Jews (21:18-40).

Paul was able then to escape from death, but the Jews continued to scheme to kill him. Then the commander arranged for Paul to be transferred to Caesarea, to Felix the governor. Later the Jews sought the favor of the newly appointed Roman governor Festus, entreating him to summon Paul to Jerusalem from Caesarea so that they could set an ambush to do away with Paul on the way. This new official, in order to please the Jews, inquired of Paul if he were willing to go up to Jerusalem to be judged there. Paul immediately answered that he would appeal to Caesar because only Caesar could judge him. This was absolutely in accordance with the Roman law because Paul was born a Roman citizen. Once he replied in this way, no one could lay a hand on him to kill him. The Roman officials had to keep him in safe custody while he waited to be sent up to Caesar (25:1-12). This is the case recorded in Acts. Our situation was similar to that of Paul; we had no other recourse. We saw the advertisements of the books before they were published and made telephone calls to the publishers, but they ignored us. After the publication of the books, we wrote hundreds of letters to them, but they still ignored us. We did not have any other way or method to reach them. We had been forced to the limit so that we had to learn of Paul to appeal to Caesar. This was not a matter of our trying to sue others. Rather, to use an illustration, we were like those who had robbers in our house. We pleaded with them to leave us, yet they would not; thus, we were forced to ask the police to come and handle the situation. This was the start of the lawsuit. Through some of the co-workers' diligent labor, we searched meticulously and were able to find the initial and early drafts of the evil books, one of which attacked Brother Nee. It was obvious that our opponents had intended to damage the Lord's recovery.

With regard to the first book, after both sides had undergone numerous depositions, the opposing party admitted that they had indeed violated the law, so to settle the matter they publicly apologized through the newspapers and also withdrew the book. With the second book, after undergoing four years of deposition, the opposing party was unable to agree among themselves; hence, the case finally went to court. Based upon the deposition material and testimonies of some expert witnesses, the judge ruled in our favor, condemning the other party of committing libel. The judgment summary was thirty-two pages long, listing more than ten important points that described how the opposite party had committed various violations. This was all based upon the depositions of both parties with proof of evidence, with both the judge and the court stenographer also verifying the record and the proceedings. As a result, the opposing party confessed and conceded defeat.

The internal problems and the external troubles caused much damage to the work of the Lord's recovery, especially in limiting its spread and increase. Nevertheless, this opposition also undeniably issued in the shining forth of the truth of the Lord. For example, in the first case against the evil book *The Mindbenders,* the lawyer undertaking the case for the opposers was a very good one. One day at the end of the deposition while everyone was still present, the lawyer said that in order to handle the case, he had to keep 12,000 pages of our writings in his memory. For this reason, he had to buy a whole set of our books. Praise the Lord! Ultimately, the truth prevails.

COMPLETING THE WORK OF INTERPRETING
THE NEW TESTAMENT

By 1973 and 1974 I began to have the sense that there was still a lack in putting out the intrinsic truths in the Lord's recovery. Brother Nee and I had co-labored together for eighteen years. I knew the riches in him and his heart's desire very well. He had released many messages; however, the majority of them had not been put into print. As a result, we have suffered a great loss. Today the number of writings by Brother Nee remaining among us is quite limited. Learning a lesson from this failure in the past, I felt that we could not go on in the way we were taking; otherwise, the truths that would remain among us would definitely be inadequate.

Hence, in accordance with the development of the work of the Lord's recovery in America, we began in 1974 to have large-scale life-study trainings twice a year, once in the winter and once in the summer. The number attending the training was always between three to four thousand; and the duration of the training was ten days. In this way, thirty messages were released each time. Our goal was to finish the study of the entire New Testament. Thank the Lord that He has truly blessed this matter, having completed this very thing.

Preparation for the trainings was not easy. Since there was one such training every six months, generally I needed two and a half to three months, a period of almost one hundred days, to write the footnotes for the New Testament. Under my leadership, several brothers who were capable in English and quite good in Greek re-translated the New Testament text. Following that, I revised it and made decisions regarding the truth. We called this new translation of the English New Testament the Recovery Version. Then based upon this new translation, I finished writing the footnotes. The preparation work included not only the revision of the scriptural text and the writing of the footnotes but also the writing of the outlines for the training messages. Then after the ten-day training, what I had spoken in the training, which had been videotaped and tape-recorded live, was put into print.

My burden in fellowshipping these few matters is so that you all may know what we went through in the past years. Now we all know that the twenty-seven books of the New Testament not only have a new translation of the text but also have footnotes and references, plus twelve to thirteen hundred accompanying messages. For the completion of this work of interpreting the entire New Testament, we truly rejoice. This has been an important work in the Lord's recovery.

REASONS FOR PROMOTING THE CHANGE OF SYSTEM

The Lord's recovery among us began in the Far East, with

mainland China as the first cradle and Taiwan as the second. In Taiwan the Lord blessed His recovery greatly so that within a few years there was a hundredfold harvest, from four or five hundred people to forty or fifty thousand people. Today on the island of Taiwan, the number of people baptized has probably exceeded 100,000. Nonetheless, we have observed that in the last decade or so there has not been much expansion or advancement. Hence, we have already begun to pay attention to this matter and have also fellowshipped with the co-workers in Taiwan that we should take heed to improve the work in Taiwan or else we will go backward. In our constant observation, although our condition truly has been worrisome, we have been following the leading of the Lord according to His timetable. At the completion of my writing of the footnotes for the entire New Testament, I put down my pen and returned to Taiwan.

After my return, I observed all kinds of situations and realized the need to have some thorough fellowship with you all. First, with the completion of the work on the entire New Testament, we can say that the truths among us truly are abundantly rich; moreover, they have all been published as books. Those who have read them can witness to the riches. Second, I hope that we would all realize that we, especially those in the Far East, have not been using the truths very much. Rather, it has been the outside Christian organizations that have been using our publications to a great degree. According to the latest estimation of the Taiwan Gospel Bookroom, the volume of sales to outside Christian organizations was at least one-third of the total. Furthermore, their favorite purchases are publications that expound the Bible, such as the life-studies and the Recovery Version of the New Testament. This proves that they have been using the riches; in contrast, our own usage has not been so thorough.

Third, the Lord's recovery among us began with Brother Nee. He truly had a clear vision. In his book *The Normal Christian Church Life,* his word on home meetings is very clear (*Collected Works of Watchman Nee,* Vol. 30, pp. 167-171). Unfortunately, even though he clearly presented these points to us early on, we have never seriously practiced them.

Fourth, our meetings everywhere have come to a standstill. In Taipei there has even been a tendency to regress. The Lord began His work in Taiwan in 1949 with one meeting hall. During the next five years the number of saints grew to such an extent that there was the need for more and more meeting halls. As the number of saints grew, small groups for shepherding were formed in each meeting hall. In the first five years, these groups were a great help to the increase of the church, resulting in the addition of a good number of people. Furthermore, a good number of the saints that were added, if not all, remained.

However, in the past ten or so years, these small groups gradually disappeared although we still had the bigger home meetings. In 1975 and 1976 Taipei had almost one hundred such meetings, of which at least seventy or eighty participated in the breaking of bread. As time passed, the home meetings were gradually combined and moved into the meeting halls. In other words, we have been gradually slipping away from the light and practice that the Lord had given us in the recovery. Since the degree of decline was very small, not precipitous, we did not even notice that we were going downhill. There is an ancient saying: "A slight error in the beginning results in a big mistake in the end." Even though we had gone off just a little, as time passed that little mistake became tremendous.

By 1984 the situation of the churches in Taiwan in general was one of everyone attending large meetings on the Lord's Day with one speaking and all the rest listening. In short, the regular large meetings were no different from the so-called worship services in degraded Christianity. This situation forced me to return anew to the New Testament, to once more study carefully all the verses related to Christian meeting from Matthew to Revelation. The light within me that the situation in Christianity was altogether different from the genuine Christian meetings portrayed in the Bible became even clearer; Christians have altogether fallen into the custom of "going to church." Among us, at least seventy percent of the saints, if not one hundred percent, have just been "going to church." This is the reason why we have not been able to spread or increase.

In October 1984 I returned to Taipei to hold a special conference for all of Taiwan, speaking on the increase of Christ. The Lord showed us that the reason the church could not spread or increase was due to several serious errors. One of these errors was that of holding large meetings so people could "go to church." If the church life is focused on the large meetings for so-called worship services, it will be difficult to continue expanding. These kinds of large meetings for worship services inhibit the truth from entering into the saints, thus making it hard for the saints to grow in life, to be built up together into the Body, and even more to function. If these matters are difficult, then bringing others in as the increase, retaining them, and holding them will be even more difficult. From that time on, this light among us has become very clear.

THE FUTURE OUTLOOK

The Need for Changing the System

In any event, the conclusion from our fellowship was first that the Lord's recovery has spread. Up to the present time, the number of people among us has not been huge, but without a doubt, the Lord's recovery has reached all of the major languages. Our literature has been translated into almost twenty languages. We may say that our publications can be found in every major language. Also, on the six continents on the earth, there are over six hundred churches in the Lord's recovery as our fields of labor. The truths and the fields for our labor are the factors of blessing in our advancement.

Consider Taipei as an example. The entire city of Taipei is our work place. Already there are twenty-one meeting halls, and the number attending the meetings is about three to four thousand. However, though there are so many people, they have not been able to function nor have they been fully put to use. This is because our system has been faulty, causing the brothers and sisters to be limited in their usefulness. We may use a country as an illustration. To have a strong country there needs to be a strong public educational system. If the educational system in the country is not sufficiently strong and widespread, then the country will have a difficult time forging ahead since it will not be able to produce talented people.

Therefore, in Taipei there was a change in the system. Everything was rearranged to open up a new atmosphere so that every place could become a workplace and a place of blessing. Regrettably, there have not been enough people to meet the need of this situation. This is because even though there are many people in the church, not many have been perfected. This was our mistake in the past, an error in our direction. For example, suppose there were some brothers who had begun meeting with us in 1949. At that time they were still single. Thirty years have since passed, and even their children have grown and now have a college education; some are even married. However, these brothers, meeting week by week, listening to messages continuously for thirty years, have not yet graduated from spiritual elementary school.

This shows us that if a person gets saved and begins to go to the meeting hall to listen to the preaching of the word, after one year, he may feel he has gotten something. However, after another year of listening, he may feel about the same; after ten or fifteen years, he will still feel almost the same. Even after hearing messages for twenty or thirty years, he will still be about the same. It seems that he understands addition, he has heard about subtraction, and he has also heard about algebra, geometry, and calculus. Yet when the time comes to apply what he has heard, he cannot add, subtract, multiply, or divide correctly, much less do calculus. The reason is that he has not gone to school to obtain a formal education. Every Lord's Day he has gone to the meeting, but at the meetings there are only some "famous" speakers preaching without any classes for learning. If at a university there were no exams, no books, and no professors but only a bunch of students listening to famous people lecturing every day, then after thirty years of listening, these students would still have not been perfected. Therefore, we must see that this has been our negligence.

This is our urgent, present need. The system for our meetings needs to be changed and must be changed. Our concepts must also be changed. The truths we preach may be spiritual, without any emphasis on education; however, since they are truths, there inherently is a good deal of substance that is educational in nature. Since it is educational, there needs to be an educational system.

The Availability and Spread of the Truth

Second, in recent years there has been a wonderful situation. Regardless of the country, the most seeking ones among the Christians have been the young people. This is a situation we did not encounter before in the past fifty years in the Lord's work. It is easy for young people to be saved, and after being saved, they have a desire for the truth. In other words, the young people all have a desire for knowledge. Since they have believed into the Lord Jesus, they want to know what He is all about and what the Bible teaches. This is why, according to the statistics of the Taiwan Gospel Bookroom, the best-selling books have been the books on studying the Bible, especially the life-studies. This phenomenon is the same throughout the world. Apparently it has not been very dramatic; however, the result and effect has been deep and wide.

In the past, the charismatic movement was quite prevailing in America, but now it is out-of-date. The charismatic movement pumps air into people, but regardless of the type of air, eventually it dissipates. Even if the best tire or the best football is filled with air, after a period of time, that air will seep out. Therefore, the charismatic movement cannot meet people's needs. What people really need today is the truth. God desires that all men would be saved and come to the full knowledge of the truth (1 Tim. 2:4). It was not only so during Paul's time but it is even more so today. The entire earth needs the truth. Take South America for example. All of Central and South America have opened to the truth, especially to the truth among us. Even if we were to send two hundred full-time workers to Central and South America, that would not be enough. Everywhere there is a reverberating cry for the truth.

If every one of our co-workers were able to present the truth to others, then wherever they went, they would be able to set up a stall for the truth. Perhaps ten people would come

on the first night, the next night twenty would come, and after
one week perhaps two hundred would come. They would all
come to listen to the truth. It is a pity that none of us goes out
to do this. We all know that the Central and South Americas
are strongly influenced by Roman Catholicism. Catholicism
does not have the truth. Although the charismatic movement
brought in some excitement for awhile, ultimately there was
no truth in it. As a result, the people in Central and South
America are hungry inwardly, longing for someone who can
preach the truth to come to them.

After this fellowship, I believe that we all will realize that
the Lord's recovery has a vast field for the work today. Furthermore, because the truths in the entire New Testament
have been completely released and put into print, we surely
have the truths among us. We should have a hope for the present generation; this refers to the young people's being saved.
Fifty years ago when we first came out to work, we did not
see a situation like the one today. Once in Taipei, after two
days of meeting, Hall One alone had about one hundred fifty
people baptized with the majority being young people. Today
the situation in the entire Lord's recovery is the same.
Whether it is in Germany, Japan, or America, everywhere
there are young people; what they seek after the most is the
truth. Today as we work, we must learn the secret that
although many things can excite the young people, what
retains them, gives them long-lasting satisfaction, and edifies
them is the truth. Therefore, first we should change the
system of our meetings by splitting them up, and second, we
should pay attention to the availability and spread of the
truth.

The Lord's recovery has already been among us for sixty
years, first entering into the Chinese-speaking world and then
moving into the English-speaking world in the west. Today
the Lord's word is in all the major languages in the world.
Our publications are even in the Russian-speaking world;
there are over ten books already translated into Russian. This
situation truly causes us to be encouraged. The speed of our
translation has not been able to match the pressing need.
This shows us that the field of work there is vast. Their

desire to seek the truth is urgent. Now we need to have a clear vision so that we can measure up to the biblical way. At the same time our goal is to present and dispense the truth.

Not only is there an abundance of truth among us, but the spiritual truths are also rich in the following four aspects: Christ, the Spirit, life, and the Body of Christ, which is the church. Aside from us, almost no one can speak on these four great truths—Christ, the Spirit, life, and the church. Among us, these truths are very rich. Today the reason we are here is because we all have been kept by the truth and have been inwardly enriched with life. Now we need to find a way to spread outwardly, allowing the Lord to truly increase.

For our practice, in principle we have to break up the large meetings into smaller meetings. This is not to say that there will not be the large meetings. Rather, on the one hand, we may have the large meetings, but on the other hand, we have to pay attention to the release and spread of the truth. For this reason, all of us must rise up to learn the truth.

Chapter Two

GOD AND THE WORD

BEING GATHERED INTO THE LORD'S NAME

In Matthew 18:20 the Lord Jesus said, "For where there are two or three gathered into My name, there am I in their midst." This is very meaningful. Apparently, all our meetings are initiated by us and are out of our own volition. Actually, they are initiated by the Lord and arranged under His sovereignty. It seems that we voluntarily come together because we hear about a meeting and take the initiative to attend it. In reality, we have to admit that our Lord is the sovereign Lord. Our meetings are not initiated by us but arranged by the Lord who is the Lord of lords and who is over all. Without Him as the Lord, we could not come from so many different places to meet together. We have to see that this is all His sovereign arrangement.

Suppose three of us want to meet together. If an earthquake occurs where I live, or if a typhoon arises where you are, or if something happens to the other brother on his way here, then we would be unable to meet together. This is only to mention events that occur outside our personal lives. Concerning matters on a more personal level, I may become sick, or there may be trouble in your family, or the other brother's company may require him to work overtime. In such cases we would still be unable to come together even though we have the desire to do so.

These examples show us that even the meeting together of only two or three persons is initiated not by us but by the Lord. It is the Lord who assembles us and gathers us together. Matthew 18:20 does not say, "Where two or three gather...." In other words, the verse is not in the active voice. Rather, it says, "Where there are two or three gathered"; it is in the passive voice. Therefore, it is not we who gather ourselves to meet; rather, it is the Lord who gathers us together.

Not only so, we are also gathered into His name. For instance, suppose there is a brother who runs a shop. If his business is very busy, so busy that he cannot get away, he most likely will not come to the meeting. However, the Lord Jesus who is in him may stir in him continually so that finally he comes to the meeting instead of remaining in his store. Who is prompting him to come? Is it he himself or is it someone else? Actually, it is neither; it is the Lord Jesus. The reason that we can come together is altogether because the Lord gathers us together; furthermore, He gathers us into His name.

I hope that from now on we all would see that every time we come together, we do not come on our own. If we still say that we come on our own to meet, then our way of speaking is too traditional and religious. We have to say that we are gathered, we are assembled. We do not take the initiative to come, but we are moved to come. It is the Lord Jesus who initiates, and it is He who stirs in every one of us and thus gathers us together.

MAN HAVING AN INNER NEED TO SEEK AFTER GOD

Now we would like to look at a topic—God and the word. Concerning God and the word, we need to speak about four matters: God being the word, the way God speaks, God's desire for us to speak, and the way to speak in the meetings. God's speaking, the way God speaks, God's desire that we speak, and our speaking in the meetings are four crucial matters to us. Simply put, these four matters are: God and the word, God being the word, God's speaking, and the word of God.

We have to spend some time to consider what the meaning of the universe is. Today many people do not know God. However, during the past six thousand years of human history, from ancient times to the present, man has never been able to break away from what is known as religion. What is religion? Religion is related to the worship of God. According to the

Chinese language, the word *religion* means having a certain belief and teaching according to that belief. To teach people what one adheres to or believes in is to practice religion.

In Acts 17 when Paul went to Athens and saw the situation there, he said to the Athenians, "I observe that in every way you very much revere your deities" (v. 22). In the original Greek language, *revering your deities* means being religious. What Paul meant was: "Men of Athens, you are very religious." This surprised me because the Greeks are famous for being intellectual, and the Greek philosophy is especially well-known for being very intellectual. Intellectual people are usually not religious or superstitious, yet the ancient Greeks were very intellectual on the one hand and also very religious on the other hand.

All human beings, regardless of whether they are intellectual or emotional, refined or rough, educated or uneducated, have an innate desire to worship God. To illustrate, every one of us has a stomach. Regardless of race or nationality, everyone who is human has a stomach, an organ specifically for containing food. In the same manner, everyone who is human has an inner need to seek after God.

GOD CREATING MAN WITH A SPIRIT TO CONTAIN HIM

The stomach in our body gives rise not only to the need to eat but also to the need to cook. We need to cook and to eat because we have a stomach. In the same way, why do we believe in God? Why do we need God? It is because we have a "stomach" to contain God, just as we have a stomach to contain food. This "stomach" for containing God is called the spirit, which was created especially for man when God created him.

Zechariah 12:1 says, "Jehovah, who stretches forth the heavens and lays the foundations of the earth and forms the spirit of man within him." This shows that Jehovah not only stretches forth the heavens and lays the foundations of the earth but also forms the spirit of man within him. This indicates that these three items—the heavens, the earth, and man—are equally important. Furthermore, instead of saying "forms man," the verse says, "forms the spirit of man within him." This clearly indicates that the emphasis is not on man but on the spirit of man. Therefore, strictly speaking, the heavens, the earth, and the spirit are of equal importance. God created the heavens, the earth, and the human spirit which distinguishes us from the animals. If we human beings did not have a spirit within, then we would be no different from the animals. We are different from animals because we have a spirit created by God.

Since the beginning of history, there have never been any sheep, dogs, or any other animals that have worshipped God or made an idol for worship. However, throughout human history from the ancient ages to the present, in human communities that were either civilized or barbaric, intelligent or foolish, rich or poor, there has been no lack of temples and idols for man to worship. This is because God created a spirit in man, and man therefore has a need to worship God.

In 1953 or 1954 an English newspaper in the Philippines reported a story about Lavrenti Beria, the chief secret agent during the rule of the former Soviet leader Stalin. According to this report Beria had murdered innumerable people during Stalin's rule. After Stalin passed away, however, Kruschev took power and immediately arrested Beria in order to execute him. When Beria was on the execution field, the execution officer told him, "Now I will give you a few minutes of freedom; whatever you ask for will be granted." Incredibly, the request of this heinous sinner before he was executed was, "Please give me a Bible." It is amazing that a chief secret agent who killed thousands of people would request to have the Bible before his execution. This story proves that deep within man there is a desire to worship God.

There is an ancient Chinese saying: "When a man is dying, his words are good." Actually, the good that is in the human heart is due to the fact that man has a spirit. There is an ancient Chinese book called *The Great Learning,* which says that the principle of great learning is to develop the "bright virtue." What is the bright virtue? The bright virtue is the conscience of man. To develop the bright virtue is to make manifest or to magnify the human conscience. The conscience is a part of the human spirit. Paul said in the New Testament that he exercised himself to always have a conscience without offense toward God and men (Acts 24:16). Therefore, within man there is something called the spirit. Like the stomach, the human spirit is an organ; the human spirit is an organ to contain God.

In the New Testament the Lord told His disciples to take Him in as food (John 6:55-57). Concerning this matter, the unbelievers, and even the Christians—the believers in the Lord, do not understand how they can eat God as food. In John 6 the Lord Jesus said, "I am the bread of life....He who eats Me, he also shall live because of Me" (vv. 35, 57). The concept of eating the Lord is not in our natural mentality. Instead, it is revealed in God's word and is gradually worked into us over a period of time.

In the spring of 1958, I spoke for the first time on the Lord Jesus being edible. The message was based on John 6:57 where the Lord said, "He who eats Me, he also shall live because of Me." After hearing that message, a saint, who was a professor at National Taiwan University and who usually was very hungry for the truth and zealous for the church, came to me and said, "This message was very good, but using such an expression as 'eating the Lord' sounds a little barbaric. How can we 'eat' the Lord?" I pointed out to him that this was what the Lord Himself said and that this was neither invented nor created by me but was recorded in the Scriptures.

In the book of Numbers the people of Israel were told that if they feared and trusted in Jehovah, then He would give their enemies to them as food (14:9). When the children of Israel entered into Canaan, they indeed "ate" their enemies. The New Testament also says something similar to this. In 1 Peter 5:8 Peter says, "Your adversary, the devil, as a roaring lion, walks about, seeking someone to devour." Satan is on earth seeking someone not to deceive but to devour. He does not only want to deceive us; rather, he wants to devour us. Therefore, we must not wait for Satan to devour us. We have to tell Satan, "You roaring lion, slow down a little. I will eat you first. Within me I have a spirit which you do not have; I will eat you up first."

ILLUSTRATIONS OF VARIOUS KINDS
OF PEOPLE SEEKING GOD

We must see that God is man's greatest need; man simply cannot rid himself of such a need. You should by no means believe the words of the atheists, who are full of deceit. With their mouths they say that there is no God, yet they secretly build up religion. More than forty years ago during World War II, Germany had a very strong military and began frequent attacks on the Soviet Union. The United States was very concerned about this. In a meeting with Stalin, the head of the Soviet Union, President Roosevelt expressed his desire that the Soviet Union allow churches within its territories to open their doors so that the believers could go to worship God. Only if this was done would the United States be able to give monetary aid to the Soviet Union. This was most likely because the money in America was coming from the taxpayers, a great number of whom were Christians and who would not agree to having the money they contributed used to help the Soviet Union, which was an atheistic country opposing God.

The Soviet leaders considered that if America would not help the Soviet Union, then sooner or later the Soviet Union would be conquered by Germany. Moreover, they probably thought that since they had persecuted Christians for over twenty years already, almost all of the Christians had probably been eliminated. They may have believed that even if the doors of the churches were re-opened, there probably would not be many who would go to church. Therefore, the Soviet Union told the United States that it would not oppose Christianity, that it would not oppose God, and that the United States should send the American dollars to them. Thus, when the Soviets opened the doors of the churches to the Christians, the help from America also arrived. It is reported that in the spring of that year, to their surprise, on the day they opened the doors of the churches, traffic was heavy and the streets were crowded with people going to worship in the churches. Stalin was greatly shocked because twenty years had passed from the time Lenin began persecuting Christianity and closing the doors of the churches to the time the doors were re-opened. Yet the number of Christians was still so great.

It is amazing that the more you persecute people and prohibit them from seeking after God, the more they will seek after God. If someone oppresses us and forbids us to eat, in the end we would surely love to eat even more. After a person has been starved for a few days, he just wants to eat. In the same way, the more you suppress people, restraining them from believing in God, the stronger will be their inner longing for God. Take mainland China for example. Over thirty years ago in China the number of Christians, including Catholics, was not more than three million, but today, in less than forty years, these three million have increased by about seventeen times to over fifty million. Therefore, to suppress people's belief in God is futile.

MAJOR RELIGIONS AMONG THE HUMAN RACE

All these illustrations tell us that within man there is something created by God. God created the heavens and the earth, and He also created a spirit within man. These three—the heavens, the earth, and the human spirit—are three outstanding items. Although most men do not know God, they have built up a living and culture of worshipping God. Therefore, we may say that the history of the human race is a history of building up religions; human beings are continually researching religions. There are only a few major religions among the human race. Further analysis and study show that all genuine religions, in principle, have only one source. First, Confucianism, strictly speaking, is not a religion. In the Confucian mentality there is only the concept of heaven, as reflected in the saying, "He who offends heaven has none to whom he can pray." Confucianism does not teach people to worship God; rather, it teaches people to be ethical and to have a purpose in life. Therefore, the followers of Confucius did not introduce a religion to mankind.

Second, in Buddhism there is no God—only Buddha, and its emphasis is on transmigration, or reincarnation. For example, someone may have been a pig in his previous life. Now in this life he has become a man. If, however, in this life he does not do good deeds, then in the next life he will become something worse than a man. However, if he does do good deeds in this life, he might become a Buddha and go to the western heaven. There is no God at all in Buddhism. Therefore, Buddhism is a way of thinking that teaches people to refrain from doing evil, because if a person does evil things, he will be punished. At the same time, it also teaches people to do good deeds and to accumulate them as much as possible. Hence, Buddhism has a certain kind of belief and teaches people according to its belief.

Taoism is even more difficult to understand. Taoism speaks about the wind, saying that the wind is like a breath and comparing human life to the wind or a breath. Thus, Taoism does not talk about God either. Therefore, neither Confucianism nor Buddhism nor Taoism talks about God. Now let us look at Christianity and Islam. Christianity includes Catholicism, Protestantism, and elements of Judaism. Chronologically, first there was Judaism, then Catholicism, and finally Protestantism. The totality of these three is Christianity. In Christianity there is a Bible with the Old Testament and the New Testament. Judaism only acknowledges the Old Testament, whereas Catholicism and Protestantism acknowledge both the Old Testament and the New Testament. In Christianity the Bible is the book that talks about God.

Islam was derived in part from the Holy Word of God. We say this because its founder, Mohammed, who was born about six hundred years after the Lord Jesus, compiled the Koran by copying from the Old Testament and part of the New Testament. Therefore, the Koran of the Islamic religion may be considered an imitation of the Old and New Testaments.

GOD AND THE WORD

From these five major religions we see that in the universe there is only one God and only one Bible. Since the Koran of the Islamic religion came from copying the Bible, it is of the same one source. This source is what the Bible calls the unique true God. Much of the human race uses this Bible, and almost all people use the calendar of this God. In other words, the building up and the development of Christianity and

Islam, were derived from this God and this Bible; that is, they were derived from God and the Word of God.

All intellectuals acknowledge that human society is a mystery, that the universe is also a mystery, and that in this mystery there is a center of reality, which is God. The expression of this God is the word; all the elements of this God are in His word. Where there is God, there is the word. Where there is no God, there is no word. It is the same with us human beings. Where there is man, there is the word. Man not only speaks, but he speaks daily. Because man has the innate ability to speak, he does not feel that to speak is precious or marvelous. But the fact that man is able to speak is an amazing thing. Animals such as cows, horses, and dogs cannot talk; they can only make sounds but no words. Therefore, man's ability to speak is a marvelous matter.

MAN HAVING A SPIRIT AND THE ABILITY TO SPEAK

When God created man, the most marvelous thing was that He created a spirit within man. Of all the millions of things God created, man alone has a spirit within him. The Chinese frequently use the word *ling* (spirit), which has many denotations. A person who is quick-minded is described as *ling-huo,* "spirit-living"; a medicine that is very effective is called *wan-ling-tan,* an "all-spirit-pill." In the Chinese culture the spirit is a special thing. The ancient Chinese sages did not teach religion, nor did they teach the worship of God. Neither did they teach people that there is a spirit in man that is a vessel to contain God. Nevertheless, they found out that in man there is something marvelous. Therefore, the Chinese say that man is the spirit of all creation. In God's creation of man, the second marvelous thing was that man was given the ability to speak. Speech does not involve only the use of the vocal cords, but it also involves the hearing of the ear and the conveying and understanding of the mind. Therefore, speech is a great, wide field of learning. Today the earth is filled with all kinds of human languages. According to some studies, the best languages are Chinese, English, Greek, and Hebrew; the latter two were used by God in revealing His word. However, in rhythm and rhyme, Greek is inferior to

Chinese. As to English, a large portion of the language follows the Greek language.

THE SPEAKING OF MAN BEING
A MANIFESTATION OF HIS LIKENESS TO GOD

All men possess two marvelous things: one is the spirit and the other is the ability to speak. Human living is altogether a story of speaking. The thing we do the most in our daily life is speak. Even if we do not do anything the whole day, we are still full of words. Suppose our ability to speak is taken away from us so that neither you nor I can speak, and neither the old nor the young can speak. If such a group of people came together, it would be hard for them to accomplish anything. Therefore, speaking is truly a tremendous matter.

We were born into a realm of speaking, we live in a realm of speaking, and we are accustomed to being in a realm of speaking. We spend our whole life in this realm, yet we do not quite realize the importance of speaking. Speaking is a crucial matter; only God Himself can give us the ability to speak. God is a speaking God, and in creating man as a vessel to contain Him and be useful to Him, He created man exactly the same as He, even to the extent that man speaks as God speaks. Therefore, man's ability to speak is a manifestation of man's likeness to God. The Bible says that God created man in His image, and the most important aspect of God's image is that God speaks; thus, man also speaks.

This matter of speaking is most frequently seen in a family. Those who are married all know that in a typical family the wife speaks more than the husband. The husband usually sits and observes, but the wife unceasingly takes care of various matters and gives orders, so naturally she speaks more. However, if the wife does not say a word the whole day, then it will be hard for the husband and the wife to live together. In the present age everyone has to learn to speak, and the more one speaks, the better he can speak. The Chinese say, "What is truly within will be manifested without." This means that if a person desires to speak weightily and properly, he must read many classic books and be fully educated. Then the words he utters can be accepted and admired by others.

GOD BEING THE WORD

Speaking is surely a marvelous thing. We need to realize that not having the Word of God is equivalent to not having God Himself. By the Lord's mercy, since the day I was saved, I have loved the Bible. For more than sixty years I have been reading the Bible every day. The more I read it, the more I sense that the Bible is lovable and precious and that what has been written in it is so marvelous and mysterious. I spent eleven and a half years to reconsider every word in the twenty-seven books of the New Testament, comparing it with the Greek text. I also made revisions to the English translation, and wherever possible I wrote footnotes for each verse. After these processes, my admiration and appreciation of the Bible have increased to the uttermost. No man could have spoken such profound and mysterious words. Only the Lord Jesus could have uttered such words to us.

The reason these words are so profound and mysterious is that the Word of God is just God Himself. We know that the words we speak are just ourselves. For instance, our voice always represents us; this is a marvelous thing. Although there are billions of people on the earth, there are not any two people who have exactly the same voice. In speaking, everyone has his own particular voice, tone, manner, and wording; even more, each is distinctly different in expression. After a person has given a message, no one else can duplicate it because the words of a person are just the person himself.

The Bible says that God is the Word (John 1:1). Apparently, the Bible does not directly say that God is the Word. However, if we study the Greek text of the Bible or the English versions, we can see that John 1:1 says, "In the beginning was the Word, and the Word was with God, and the Word was God." Here, *the Word was God* in Greek is "God was the Word." Whether it is "God was the Word" or "the Word was God," they are actually the same. For example, we can either say that Mr. Chen is Brother Chen or that Brother Chen is Mr. Chen; there is no difference. Saying that your wife is Mrs. Chang and saying that Mrs. Chang is your wife are both acceptable since both refer to her as your wife.

In the Bible there is such a verse which says, "In the beginning was the Word, and the Word was with God, and the Word was God" (John 1:1). This is a great verse showing us that the Word and God are one. The Word is God, and God is the Word. Likewise, we can say that man is the word, and the word is man. Before this we might have never thought of ourselves as being the word. Although many animals can make certain vocal sounds, they cannot speak and do not have words. Only man has words; hence, man is the word. If someone wants to know what I am thinking within, he has to know it through my words. Therefore, when we come to the Bible, we come to God, because the Bible as the Word is God Himself.

GOD SPEAKING

Not only is God the Word, but He also speaks; furthermore, He created men who speak. God is the Word, but if He did not speak, He would not be the Word. Because God is the Word, He speaks. We may use a preacher as an illustration. The life of a preacher is a life of words because over the months and years he speaks unceasingly to people. The book of Hebrews tells us that our God is a speaking God; He not only spoke in old times, but He is still speaking today. Formerly, He spoke through the prophets to our forefathers; today He speaks to us in His Son, that is, in Himself, and He speaks to us from within us (Heb. 1:1-2).

The Lord Jesus said to Philip, "Do you not believe that I am in the Father and the Father is in Me? The words that I say to you I do not speak from Myself, but the Father who abides in Me does His works" (John 14:10). This shows us that the Lord Jesus' speaking was God's working. In other words, the Lord's speaking was God's speaking; the Lord and God are one. Today our God is still speaking, and He speaks in His Son. We all are the members of the Body of His Son; thus, when we speak, it is God speaking in His Son. When we preach the gospel, it is God speaking in the Son.

Speaking can cause things, even big things, to happen. When the people of the world do business, their success or failure depends on whether or not they know how to speak. Before going out, a salesperson has to be taught and trained in speaking. Those who know how to talk will get the business, and those who talk improperly or inadequately will not get the business. Sometimes talking too much will also cause a salesperson to lose business. Therefore, all the successful salespeople are able to speak and know how to speak very well. Actually, interaction in human society depends on speaking; moreover, the speaking must be proper and suitable. Therefore, speaking causes things to happen, and it can greatly affect the outcome of a matter.

Today our working for the Lord also depends on speaking. If we speak well, people will be saved; if we speak poorly, people will not understand the gospel. If we speak well, people will be edified; if we speak poorly, our work will be futile. There is a Chinese proverb which says, "A word can cause a nation to rise; a word can cause a nation to fall." It means that the rise or fall of a nation can depend on man's speaking. We all acknowledge that God's creation of the universe was a great act. Yet this great act was accomplished by speaking. Genesis 1:3 says, "And God said, Let there be light; and there was light." Whatever God spoke came into existence. Therefore, in the Psalms the psalmist praised God, saying, "For He spoke, and it was; / He commanded, and it stood" (33:9). If God had not spoken anything, then it would have been impossible for the universe to come into existence. Even our existence depends to a great extent on God's speaking. The Lord Jesus said, "He who hears My word and believes...has eternal life" (John 5:24). Our being saved and our receiving the eternal life are altogether dependent upon the Lord's word.

THE WORD OF GOD

Lastly, we want to look at ten major items related to the word of God.

Being Christ

First, the Word of God is Christ (John 1:1; Rev. 19:13). Who is Christ? Christ is God; hence, the Word of God is Christ.

Being the Spirit

Second, the word of God is the Spirit (John 6:63; Eph.

6:17). In John 6 the Lord Jesus told the disciples, "The words which I have spoken to you are spirit" (v. 63), and Ephesians 6 says that "the Spirit...is the word of God" (v. 17).

As Life

Third, the word of God is life. John 6 also shows us that the word of God is life. The Lord said, "The words which I have spoken to you...are life" (v. 63).

As Light

Fourth, the word of God is light. In the Old Testament the psalmist praised the Lord for His word, saying, "Your word is a lamp to my feet / And a light to my path" (Psa. 119:105). This verse is very poetic and was written according to the situation in ancient times. In ancient times there were no electrical street lights, nor were there any other kinds of light on the path. Therefore, when people walked during the night, they had to carry a lamp to illuminate their footsteps. Hence, the psalmist gave this utterance: "Your word is a lamp to my feet." The word of God is a lamp; when a person carries it while walking, it is a lamp to his feet. As such, it becomes the light on his path when he walks. The word of God is our lamp, our light. If we have the word of God, we have the light; if we do not have the word of God, we are in darkness.

As Food

Fifth, the word of God is our food. In Matthew 4:4 the Lord Jesus said, "Man shall not live on bread alone, but on every word that proceeds out through the mouth of God." A prophet in the Old Testament also said, "Your words were found and I ate them, / And Your word became to me / The gladness and joy of my heart" (Jer. 15:16). All those who love the word of the Lord can testify that God's words in them are their sweetness and joy.

As the Seed

Sixth, the word of God is the seed. We know that seeds have life. When we receive the word of God, this word enters into us and becomes a seed of life. At that very moment we are regenerated, within us there is the germination of life. First Peter 1:23 says, "Having been regenerated not of corruptible seed but of incorruptible, through the living and abiding word of God." Matthew 13:3 says that the Lord went out to sow. The seed which He sowed was the word of God. The Lord's sowing is the Lord's speaking. What does He speak? He speaks God's word; He speaks God Himself. This is the seed of life.

As the Rain

Seventh, God's word is the rain. We know that when a seed is planted into the soil, it cannot grow without the rain. This thought is clearly shown in the Scriptures. Deuteronomy tells us that God's speaking is like raindrops upon the plants and vegetables (32:2). Isaiah also said that the word of God descends from heaven and will not return to Him vainly, but rather it is like the rain and the snow which come upon the earth to water the earth and make it bear and sprout forth, so that it may give seed to the sower and bread to the eater (55:10-11). God's word is like the rainwater; for the seed to grow, it still needs to be watered with God's word as the rain. It is exceedingly marvelous that the word of God is life and also the seed of life; moreover, it is the rain that waters this seed.

As the Dew

Eighth, the word of God is the dew. Rain and dew are different. It is not sufficient for the vegetation in the field to have rain only. Therefore, in the latter part of the night, there is the descending dew (Deut. 32:2). The dew is more effective than the rain because the rainwater mostly goes to the roots, but the dew mostly descends on the leaves and branches. Everything created by God has its spiritual significance. We see that the word of God is life, the seed of life, and the rain which waters the seed; even more, it is the dew which moistens the plants.

As a Sharp Sword

Ninth, God's word is a sharp sword. A sharp sword is for fighting. Hebrews 4:12 says, "For the word of God is living...and sharper than any two-edged sword." Here the sword is used for dealing with our self to discern the thoughts and intentions of our heart, that is, to divide our soul and our spirit. The unsaved people, and even the saved ones who do not have the word of God, may confuse the soul and the spirit. However, when we quietly read the Word of God, regardless of which chapter or verse, we will be able to clearly discern our spirit from our soul.

For instance, there was a man who had a disagreement with his wife. Although both of them loved the Lord and did not quarrel, they always reasoned with one another. Sometimes they would pray, but after praying they would start reasoning again. One morning the husband was reading his Bible. What he read was not related to the matter of reasoning. It was just Psalm 19, which says, "The heavens declare the glory of God, / And the firmament proclaims the work of His hands" (v. 1). While reading it, he spontaneously prayed with the words of this verse; he prayed and read, and read and prayed. Although he did this for only ten minutes, afterward he was clear inwardly, knowing that when he prayed he was in the spirit but that when he reasoned with his wife he was in the soul. If he had not had this kind of reading and praying in the morning, the soul and the spirit within him could not have been divided. By reading the Word and praying in spirit, he was able to clearly discern his spirit from his soul. Thus, he learned a secret so that the next time he encountered a cause for reasoning, he would quickly return to his spirit to pray. The wife might reason but he would not; the more she would reason, the more he would pray. This is God's word as a sharp sword, clearly dividing our spirit and our soul.

Ephesians 6:17 also speaks about this matter. There it talks about the spiritual warfare needed to deal with the enemy. It says that the word of God is a sharp sword for slaying the enemy. Therefore, we see that God's word is a sharp sword; it slays the devil, and it also divides our spirit and our soul.

As a Hammer

Lastly, God's word is a hammer (Jer. 23:29) which breaks

to pieces our self, our hardened heart, and our opinions. Jeremiah 23:29 also says that God's word is a fire to burn us. We can see that the word of God has so many functions.

For us to live a normal life today, we must be in the word of God. On the other hand, for the church to be strong and normal, built up, spiritual, and mature in life, we must speak the word of God. What we need today is our God, who is the word. This word is in the Holy Scriptures. We must receive the word and speak the word. Thus, the word of God as Christ, as the Spirit, as life, as light, as food, as the seed, as the rain, as the dew, as a sword, and as a hammer will be manifested as a reality upon us. The word of God can do innumerable things; everything hinges on God's word. Hence, we must do all we can to read the Word of God.

CHAPTER THREE

GOD DESIRING THAT MAN SPEAK FOR HIM

God is a speaking God. He created the universe and continues to do all things through His speaking. Therefore, everyone who has been saved and who has His life should learn to speak for Him and to speak His word.

The greatest mystery in the universe is God. Where is this mystery opened and revealed to man? This mystery is opened and revealed to us in His Word. Hebrews 1 tells us that our God is a speaking God (vv. 1-2). The speaking of the human race came from His creation. He is a speaking God, and He is also the Word.

We have already seen that the Lord's word is the Lord Himself, the Spirit, life, light, food, the seed of life, the rain that waters the seed, and the dew that moistens the plant. The Lord's word is everything to us. The problem, however, is that we, the people of God, still have Satan and the flesh with us. Moreover, sometimes because we are confused, we mix up the spirit and the soul and are unable to discern one from the other. Therefore, God's word is also a sharp sword which defeats Satan for us, divides our spirit from our soul, and deals with our flesh. Not only so, the word of God is like a big hammer carrying out a breaking work in us.

MAN CREATED IN THE IMAGE OF GOD

Now let us go a step further to see God's desire, which is that man speak for Him. This matter sounds easy to understand, but it contains a biblical mystery. God shows us clearly in the Bible that His purpose in creating man was that man might speak for Him. Genesis 1:26 says, "God said, Let Us make man in Our image, according to Our likeness." This was spoken during a council of the Divine Trinity to determine how to create man. The result was that God made man in His image. How did God create man in His image?

According to the inner-life people, *image* in Genesis 1:26 refers not to an outward form but to the attributes of God's being such as love, light, holiness, and righteousness. Love, light, holiness, and righteousness are four exceedingly great items. If we carefully study the Ten Commandments (Exo. 20:3-17), the law decreed by God, we will discover that the crucial contents of these laws are these four items: love, light, holiness, and righteousness.

The law first talks about the holiness of God, then the righteousness of God, then the love of God, and finally the light of God. It seems that in the Ten Commandments we cannot find these four great items—holiness, righteousness, love, and light; nevertheless, these four matters are the very content of the Ten Commandments. From the outset, God prohibited the people from making idols and from bowing down to them; He also told them that they should not take the name of Jehovah in vain and that they should remember the Sabbath day so as to sanctify it (vv. 3-11). These four commandments show us that He is the holy God, the God who is sanctified, different from all other gods, transcendent, uncommon, and distinct from all things. Therefore, the first four commandments speak of God's holiness; they were written according to God's attribute of holiness.

We know that the kind of law a person makes always expresses the kind of person he is. A good person makes good laws, and a bad person makes bad laws. If bank robbers could make laws, they would surely legalize bank robbery. The reason our God established such holy laws is because He is holy. "Honor your father and your mother....You shall not kill" (vv. 12-13)—these commandments show us that God is love. "You shall not steal" (v. 15)—this speaks of God being righteous. "You shall not testify with false testimony against your neighbor" (v. 16)—this concerns God being light. People who lie are in darkness, and those who kill and do not honor their father and mother are without love.

If we analyze the Ten Commandments, we will see that

their basic points are God's holiness, God's righteousness, God's love, and God's light. The fact that God created man in His image means that God made man according to what He is. God is holiness, righteousness, love, and light, and according to these items, God created man. Therefore, as those created by God, we also have these virtues in our nature. It is true that we are corrupt and fallen, that many evil things have been manifested through us from the time we were born to the time we have grown up, and that we have been affected by the filthiness of human society. Nevertheless, in our nature, in the depths of our being, we still have these four virtues. For example, when we love others, we feel very happy inside, and when we hate people, we feel ashamed. In the depths of man there is something of love. Furthermore, people like to do the things of light; even children are like this. No one likes to do the things of darkness. This proves that in man there is definitely the characteristic of God as light. God's creation of man in the beginning was according to His love and His light.

Everyone knows that to steal is wrong. Even though someone might feel good after he has stolen something, in him there is a sense of justice which condemns his action; this is righteousness. As human beings, we are deeply fallen and improper, yet from the time we are young, none of us wants to be a failure, despised by others. We all want to be honorable, outstanding, respected, and distinguished; this is according to the holy nature of God. This shows that within created man there are indeed these four characteristics: love, light, holiness, and righteousness.

We all know that animals do not have these characteristics and virtues; only human beings have them. Why? Because when God created man, He created him according to the image of what He is—love, light, holiness, and righteousness. It is a pity that today many Christians still do not realize that when God created man in His image, He created in man all these virtues and characteristics.

Another special matter in God's creation of man is that since God is a speaking God, when He created man in His image, He created man with the ability to speak just like Himself. Because God is a God of love, light, holiness, and righteousness, He created man with love, light, holiness and righteousness. Because God is a speaking God, He created man to be just like Him—also being able to speak.

Among the human race there is a special book—the Holy Bible. This book has always been held in the highest estimation throughout the generations. In Latin, it is called the Book of books, the unique book, or the most extraordinary book. This book has suffered opposition and has been damaged, but today it still stands upright and unshaken. On the earth today there are translations of the Bible among almost every race and in almost every tongue. The Bible has been translated into all kinds of written and spoken languages in the world. Aside from the Bible, there is no other book that has been spread universally in so many different kinds of dialects. Only the divine Word has universally reached almost every human language. In other words, God is the unique God, and the Bible is the unique word among the human race.

The Bible is among nearly every race, people, and tongue, and there are Christians among nearly every human race, people, and tongue. Therefore, the New Testament says that Christians are people who have been called "out of every tribe and tongue and people and nation" (Rev. 5:9). God has called us out of different languages. Today on this globe there is hardly a nation, people, or tongue in which there are no Christians. This is a glorious thing. In almost every people and every language in the world there are Christians and there is the Bible. When we Christians come together, although we are of different races and speak different languages, we can connect with one another in our conversations.

God is a speaking God, and when He created us, He wanted us also to speak. Not only do we have His image in love, light, holiness, and righteousness, but we also represent Him and have His image in our ability to speak. According to Genesis 1:26, God created us not only that we might have His image but even more that we might rule for Him. Therefore, He gave us the authority to have dominion over all the other creatures, that is, "over the fish of the sea and over the birds of heaven and over the cattle and over all the earth."

Inwardly in our image we are like God, having love, light,

holiness, and righteousness. Outwardly, God is a speaking God, and like Him, we also are able to speak. Among God's creatures, there are only two kinds that can speak. One kind consists of the angels in heaven. Angels do speak. Before the Lord Jesus was born, an angel came to reveal His name to Joseph (Matt. 1:20-21). Charles Wesley wrote a hymn: "Hark! the herald angels sing, / 'Glory to the new-born King'" (*Hymns,* #84). Therefore, it was an angel who spoke first, and it was an angel who announced the good news first; thereafter, we must preach the gospel.

Why is it that we human beings are able to speak? It is because we are God's representatives. He created us that we might represent Him. The most important requirement of a representative is that he must be able to speak. If today someone sends a representative to us, yet this representative, being dumb, is not able to talk, then in the end no agreement can be reached since there is no possibility of having any discussion. This kind of representative is a useless representative. Today we can represent God because we can speak. I believe that many Christians have not thought about this. We can speak because we are like God.

We have already pointed out that God created man with two outstanding features: one is that He created a spirit within man, and the other is that He created a speaking organ for man. This speaking organ is not simple; it consists of the vocal chords, the tongue, the teeth, the mouth, and the lips, all of which are for speaking. Someone might say that these parts are mainly for eating and drinking. Please consider, though, how many times a day does a person eat and how many times does he drink? Actually, the most repetitious action a person does in a day is breathing; man continuously breathes. In the Bible breathing and speaking are linked together. Concerning the Bible, 2 Timothy 3:16 says, "All Scripture is God-breathed." This means that God's speaking is linked to His breathing. Since breathing and speaking are linked together, when someone speaks, he naturally breathes. In other words, if a person cannot breathe or will not breathe, he cannot speak.

In America a certain military physician who had done

some research discovered that the exercise most beneficial to human health is deep breathing. If a person would do deep breathing frequently, he will be healthy. In God's creation no other creatures can speak as well as breathe. Only we human beings can breathe and speak as well—this is something unique. According to 2 Timothy 3:16, we speak just like God speaks. Our entire speaking apparatus is mysterious and marvelous, and it was entirely created by God. God created us with such an apparatus in order that we may be able to speak.

In the old times God spoke through the prophets in many portions and in many ways to the fathers (Heb. 1:1). Today He speaks to us in the Son (v. 2a). If we read through the sixty-six books of the Bible, we can see that the Bible contains many words of wisdom, and all the things mentioned are wonderful and comprehensive, including subjects such as astronomy, geography, science, and physics. The book of Isaiah, for example, says, "It is He [God] who sits above the circle of the earth" (40:22a). In the original Hebrew text the word *earth* is the same as the word *earth* in Genesis 1:1: "In the beginning God created the heavens and the earth." When the Scriptures were written, man did not have the concept of the earth as a "globe." As we know, the Bible was translated into Chinese at a much later time. About a hundred years ago when the Bible was translated into Chinese, Columbus had already discovered that the earth was round, not flat; therefore, the translators of the Chinese Bible could easily translate this verse into "He who sits above the circle of the earth." Before Columbus discovered the new continent, however, hardly anyone believed that the earth was round; instead, most people thought that the earth was flat. Still, more than a thousand years before Columbus, the prophet Isaiah in his book referred to the earth as a circle, saying that God sits above the circle of the earth.

From this we see that the Bible is truly a heavenly book, the record of the divine speaking. It has everything in it. It has wisdom and life, and it is all-inclusive and most mysterious. The Bible is the Word of God.

THE REGENERATED, SAVED PERSONS BEING
ABLE TO PROPHESY FOR GOD

We have already seen that God created us not only to be like Him in having love, light, holiness, and righteousness but also to be like Him in being able to speak. However, we need to know what kinds of words God wanted man to speak when He created man with the ability to speak. Did He want man merely to speak the words of man? God created man to represent Him. A representative should speak the words of the one he represents. As God's representatives, we represent God; therefore, we must speak God's words. We have to speak for God and speak forth God; this God is the word.

However, due to our fall, we were joined to Satan; thus, Satan has come into us to speak in us. The Chinese character for *soul* is formed by two radicals: one radical denotes *demon* while the other denotes *say* or *speak*. Hence, *soul* means *demon-speaking;* demon-speaking is the soul. A fallen person is a soul, and when he opens his mouth, it is often like the speaking of demons. After being regenerated in our spirit, we the saved ones are the children of God. As such, when we open our mouth, it ought to be God speaking; we speak whatever God speaks. This may be likened to someone speaking Chinese because he was born a Chinese; we speak the language of the one of whom we were born.

Since we all have been begotten of God, within us we ought to have the "God" tone; whatever we speak, we speak about God. In America there are people of different colors: white, red, yellow, brown, and black. Among these races, the Asian people are difficult to distinguish outwardly. For example, the Chinese and the Koreans look very much alike, and the Malaysians and the Indonesians also look about the same. How then does one tell the difference? It is by listening to their speech. Once they begin to talk, we know then that this one is Chinese and that one is Korean, this one is from Malaysia and that one was born in Indonesia. We speak the words of the one of whom we were born. Since we were born of God, naturally we speak God's words. Since God's word is God Himself, when we speak God's word, we speak God.

The New Testament shows us that God wants us, the saved

ones, to prophesy as prophets (1 Cor. 14:31). To prophesy is to speak the word of God instead of the word of demons or the word of man. The word of God is just God Himself; when we prophesy by speaking, we speak the word of God. Concerning this matter, Paul in the New Testament and Moses in the Old Testament (Num. 11:29) were in agreement. In 1 Corinthians 14:31 Paul said, "You can all prophesy one by one." Paul believed that every one of us can speak for God. The word *can* has two interpretations in Bible translation. The Chinese Union Version translates it into *may*. That everyone may prophesy means that everyone has the right, though not necessarily the ability, to prophesy. The Greek word has both meanings: *all may* and *all can*. Today as prophets, you and I, the saved ones, not only may but also can prophesy and speak for God.

Although we became fallen, once we are regenerated and our spirit is made alive, we are doubly able to speak for God, even more able than Adam. Adam was only created, not regenerated. Although we were created and became fallen, we have been regenerated and saved. John 1:12-13 says, "But as many as received Him, to them He gave the authority to become children of God, to those who believe into His name, who were begotten not of blood, nor of the will of the flesh, nor of the will of man, but of God." Since we have been begotten of God, we can speak the word of God. If a child is born of us and is not dumb, it is impossible for him to be unable to speak human words. Therefore, we all need to be encouraged to speak the word of God after our regeneration.

Paul told the Corinthians, "You can all prophesy one by one" (1 Cor. 14:31). The reason Paul said this is because the Corinthians, after receiving the Holy Spirit, had turned aside to pay attention to the so-called speaking in tongues. Paul seemed to be admonishing them, saying, "Why do you have to pay attention to such tongues? God has regenerated you and has made you His children to speak for Him. Since you can all prophesy one by one, why do you have to play with those strange tongues? They may be merely human-invented sounds of the tongue. What God requires of you is that you speak for Him."

Chapter fourteen of 1 Corinthians is just one chapter of the entire book. If we want to understand this chapter, we have to look at the whole book of 1 Corinthians. Chapter one of 1 Corinthians clearly shows us that Christ is wisdom, as well as power, to us from God (vv. 24, 30a). This is not only the main topic of chapter one of 1 Corinthians, it is also the focus and subject of the entire book of 1 Corinthians. God has given Christ to us as our wisdom and our power. Today whether in our daily walk or in our various activities in the church, Christ is our wisdom and our power. Therefore, in our daily speaking we speak Christ, and in our speaking in the meetings we speak Christ all the more. The prophesying mentioned in 1 Corinthians 14 refers to speaking Christ. As long as we speak Christ, we are prophets.

In the Scriptures the prophets are not ordinary people; they are people who speak for God. Those who speak the word of God are the prophets. In the Old Testament sometimes God would come upon someone, and then this one would have the word of God. When God's word came upon someone and when this one opened his mouth to speak God's word, this one was then a prophet. If a person did not have God coming upon him, and if he did not speak God or speak for God, he was merely an ordinary person. He would become a prophet, however, immediately after he opened his mouth to speak God, to speak God's words, and to speak for God. Today are we merely ordinary people or are we prophets? We have to know that in the Old Testament there were no self-appointed prophets, nor were there prophets designated by men. Rather, it was when God came upon a person, and this person spoke for God, that he was a prophet. As long as we speak for God, we are prophets. Opening our mouths to speak the word of God is the qualification for us to become prophets.

Suppose some young people have been saved for only two months, and at home they have grandparents who not only do not believe in the Lord, but who sometimes even scold them in anger. When these young people find an opportunity, they should lift up their spirit and say to their grandparents, "Do you know there is only one true God in this universe? The gods our neighbors worship are not the true God; there is only one true God." When they speak to their grandparents about God, they are prophets. They may not be experienced prophets, but at least they are little prophets. How glorious this is! Once we speak concerning God, we are speaking for God, and as long as we speak for God, we are prophets.

While Moses was leading about two million Israelites through the wilderness to enter Canaan, these people frequently murmured, created trouble, and caused disturbances until he could no longer bear it. He alone was bearing the heavy burden of leading these two million people who complained constantly; therefore, he felt that he could not bear the burden by himself. God then told him to gather from among the elders of the Israelites seventy persons and to bring them to the tent of meeting. Sixty-eight of the seventy came to the tent of meeting. These sixty-eight persons received the Spirit who was upon Moses, and they began to prophesy. The two who did not come to the tent of meeting but remained in their own tents also began to prophesy in the camp. Someone came and reported this to Moses. Joshua, Moses' helper, was not happy when he heard it, so he asked Moses to restrain them (Num. 11:1-28). Moses immediately said to Joshua, "Are you jealous for my sake? Oh that all Jehovah's people were prophets, that Jehovah would put His Spirit upon them!" (v. 29).

This shows us that Paul in the New Testament was not the only one who had this kind of vision in 1 Corinthians 14:31: "You can all prophesy one by one." It is very likely that Paul's concept came from Moses, because Paul, as one who understood the Old Testament, must have been familiar with what Moses had said in Numbers 11:29, "Oh that all Jehovah's people were prophets!" We know that when Paul wrote the Epistles in the New Testament, many of his words were derived from the Old Testament. Therefore, we see that this concept is consistent in both the Old and New Testaments—God wants His people to speak for Him.

AN IMPORTANT HISTORY OF THE PROPAGATION OF THE BIBLE

The Bible completed through the apostle was an open book

intended for all the children of God. However, Satan, who is vicious and subtle, locked up the Bible through the Roman Catholic Church. The pope gave an order saying that the Bible was too sacred and beyond the understanding of the ordinary people. Therefore, they could not read it nor interpret it; only the pope and the few archbishops under him had the ability to understand it. Therefore, the theological and doctrinal definitions in the Catholic Church were all decided through papal decrees; the common people were not permitted to make any decisions for themselves.

In a way, the most important thing accomplished through the Reformation, which is well-known in history, was not the recovery of the truth concerning justification by faith but the release of the Bible to the general public. Those who have read history know that before the Reformation, people did not have newspapers. It was during the Reformation that the reformers invented the newspaper to propagate the truth they saw. Therefore, through the Reformation the Bible was firstly unlocked and the word of God was released; secondly, the newspaper was invented as a way to propagate the word of God. Regrettably, Christians today do not utilize the newspaper to intensify the power of the gospel. On the contrary, it is the worldly people who use newspapers for the mass spread of news. This is a lamentable matter. Therefore, we have to see that where the work of the Lord is, there must also be the literature work for the spread and release of the Lord's word.

Although Martin Luther took the lead to unlock the Bible five hundred years ago, the Bible had not been fully interpreted by then. When people came to the book of Revelation, they said that this book was a mysterious book that should not be read because it was incomprehensible. Then about one hundred years ago, the Lord raised up the Brethren in England. The Bible scholars among them, with John Nelson Darby as the leader and others such as William Kelly and C. H. Mackintosh, interpreted so many of the types and prophecies in the Bible. They saw the meaning of the great human image in Daniel chapter two, the four beasts in chapter seven, and the seventy weeks in chapter nine. Through their understanding and knowledge of these three matters, they were able to open up the book of Revelation. Thus, a hundred years ago the Bible became not only a released book but also an interpreted book.

Ever since the Lord's recovery started in China, we have paid much attention to studying the truth and the Bible. We have read deeply into church history and thoroughly researched the various important schools of interpretation of the Bible. Hence, in our exposition of the Scriptures, we are standing on the shoulders of our predecessors. We may say that the Lord's recovery today has passed through Luther, Zinzendorf, the Brethren, and now it has reached us. This is why we have utterances such as "Christ is all-inclusive." This is what we have seen, and this utterance is uniquely ours. We are able to see so many things because we are standing on the shoulders of our predecessors. If I stand on the ground, what I can see will be very limited, but if I climb onto the top of a thousand-man human pyramid and stand on the shoulders of the person on the very top, then I will be able to see much farther. This is not to say that we are looking down on our predecessors; rather, we are grateful for what they saw, but at the same time, we feel that what they saw was lower. Although the things they saw were numerous, they were on the ground level. Although we have not seen as many things as they first saw, the things we have seen are high and were seen from a high position.

The reason the Bible has been opened to us today is that God wants us to speak, and He wants us to speak His word. In the history of the propagation of the Bible, the Bible was locked up at first by the Catholic Church for about one thousand years, from A.D. 500 to A.D. 1500. This period of one thousand years is called the Dark Ages in history. Why was it dark? That age was dark because there was practically no Bible, no Word of God. Then during the Reformation the Bible was released, and one hundred and fifty years ago it was interpreted through the Brethren. Today the highest theologies are based on the theological teachings of the Brethren. The theologies of the two higher schools of theology in America today—the Dallas Theological Seminary and the Moody Bible Institute—are basically those of the Brethren. Today the so-called proper and orthodox teachings of Protestant Christianity are all influenced by the teachings of the Brethren.

THE DEGRADED SYSTEM IN CHRISTIANITY
SHUTTING UP PEOPLE'S MOUTHS

Although God's desire is that we all speak for Him, today in Christianity the degraded system of worship services is a system of one man speaking and all the rest listening. Such a system of one person speaking shuts the mouths of everyone else.

Thirty years ago when I was in Manila, Philippines, working for the Lord, one of the saints had a relative who was sick and was staying in the hospital. This saint brought along two or three others to visit his relative. While they were there, some other Christian friends and relatives of the sick person also came to visit him. When the other Christians saw our brothers and sisters praying so confidently, they were astonished and asked, "Are all of you pastors?" The reason they asked this was that those Christians did not even know how to pray.

I was born into a Christian family, studied in a Christian school, and attended Sunday school every week. My mother was baptized quite early in life, so when we were young, she taught us many Bible stories. We were moved to tears when we heard the stories. However, I never once saw her pray. Even so, every Lord's Day she always insisted that we children dress up properly and go to church. We did this week after week and year after year; apart from the pastor, we did not hear anyone else who could preach or pray. Therefore, it was commonly said that if someone is sick, he should see a doctor, if he goes to court, he should get a lawyer, and if he needs prayer, he should find a pastor. In Christianity the pastors are those who specialize in prayer and Bible reading, while all the other people do not have the ability to speak.

We are speaking these things in order to show you Satan's scheme. The Bible has been released from the chains of Catholicism through Luther and interpreted through the Brethren. Yet because of the traditions of Christianity, the degraded system has produced many who belong to the clergy. These ones specialize in preaching, Bible reading, and praying, while the rest of the congregation remains silent, not needing to speak for God or to speak God's word. This is due to the fact that people have become accustomed to merely "going to church" and have thus lost their ability to speak for the Lord. This is altogether the subtlety of Satan. God wants us to speak, and He wants us to speak His word. After saving us and regenerating us, He wants us to speak for Him and to speak Him forth. Since we are begotten of God, we ought to speak God's word and to speak God. However, the concept of "going to church" in today's Christianity has shut up all the mouths of the children of God.

Therefore, in the Lord's recovery we need to change the system of our meetings. In our meetings we should not have one person speaking and the rest just listening; rather, everyone should speak. If we look at the context of 1 Corinthians 14:31, we can see that when Paul said, "You can all prophesy one by one," he was referring to speaking in the meetings. When the whole church comes together, we all can prophesy one by one, speaking for the Lord.

GOD WANTING MAN TO SPEAK GOD'S WORD
FOR GOD'S EXPRESSION

The purpose of God in creating man in His image was that man might express Him. In which points does man express Him? First, man expresses Him in speaking. There are some Christians today who believe that we can express God by our behavior alone and without speaking. In other words, they say that if we have a good testimony and a proper living with good behavior, we will be able to express God in the presence of men. This is not wrong, and this has its place, but we cannot avoid the matter of speaking for God. Speaking cannot be replaced; speaking is the real expression. Suppose there is a preacher who dresses himself tidily and properly and has his hair combed neatly, and when he stands on the podium, he is gentle and courteous, giving people the feeling that he really behaves well. However, if he would stand there for two hours, staring at the congregation with a smile but without saying a word, the congregation would not be satisfied, and he would not be able to express God. Therefore, when we express God, we need to have a proper living, but even more we need to speak forth clear words.

Regardless of whether we are in the office, in school, or in the midst of our relatives and friends, we need to speak. If we do not speak, it will not be easy for us to maintain a proper testimony. For instance, suppose you work for a certain company, but you have never told people that you are a Christian, and you refuse to let them know that you are a Christian. Rather, you only try to maintain a good conduct. In this way, perhaps after half a month, your colleagues may come and invite you to a Saturday or Sunday dancing party. Then it would be hard for you to be separated from among them. However, suppose you go to a new place to work, and after the first or second day at work, you declare, "I am a Christian; I love the Lord Jesus." After two weeks when they are planning to have a dancing party, they will not come to you, so you are naturally separated from among them. Therefore, if you do not declare and if you do not speak, you leave a back door for Satan to come in and for you to slip out. But once you have declared and spoken, not only is the back door closed, but every other door is also closed; then you have protected yourself.

God wants us to express Him mainly through our speaking for Him. In the time of Noah when the whole earth was corrupted, God came and called Noah to be a herald of righteousness (2 Pet. 2:5), and Noah then preached the righteous words of God for one hundred and twenty years. Today we should speak for God in the same way.

GOD DESIRING THAT
ALL THE PEOPLE OF JEHOVAH BE PROPHETS

Having the Full Knowledge of the Truth

How do we speak for God? To speak for God, we need to have the full knowledge of the word of God (1 Tim. 2:4). Today the main reason that Christians cannot speak for God is that they do not understand the word of God. Therefore, we need to learn to understand the word of God; then we will be able to speak for God.

Letting the Word of Christ Dwell in Us Richly

Next, we have to let the word of Christ dwell in us richly (Col. 3:16). The words *let* and *dwell* are strong words in Greek. It is not just to store the words of Christ richly in us, as the Chinese Union Version says. Here, the word of Christ is considered a living person; the word of Christ is the personified word. If we just let the word be stored in us, the word does not have to be a person. However, if we want to let the word *dwell* in us, the word must be a person. This is why Colossians says that we have to let the word of Christ *dwell* in us richly. He is waiting for us to *let* Him, and He wants to *dwell* in us; in this way we have the word of the Lord in us.

Being Experienced
in God's Word of Righteousness

Furthermore, we need to be experienced in God's word of righteousness (Heb. 5:13-14). In the book of Hebrews, the shallow word of God is called "the word of the beginning of Christ" (6:1); God's word of righteousness is deeper and more mystical. We all need to be experienced in the deeper word of God so that when needed we may have the words with which to speak for God.

Speaking the Word of God
in Season and out of Season

Finally, Paul told Timothy to proclaim the word, to speak for God, in season and out of season (2 Tim. 4:2).

THE WORD OF GOD GROWING, MULTIPLYING,
AND BECOMING STRONG

What we should emphasize after the changing of the system is teaching the saints the truth according to a certain line of lessons. At the same time, we hope that at the end of every Lord's table and every prayer meeting, we could reserve half an hour to speak a portion of God's word. In this way, every week, besides the formal learning of the truth, we will also have the two periods of time, after the prayer meeting and the Lord's table, to learn the truth. The food that the Lord has given us is so rich. The twenty-seven books of the New Testament in particular have all been interpreted for us, and the truths are quite clear. Therefore, this matter would not be too difficult.

For example, a church may be divided into four places for meetings, and each place may have two brothers who are responsible specifically to prepare for the speaking after the Lord's table. They should pray and consider one of the twenty-seven books of the New Testament, and if they think that the book of Ephesians is fitting, then they should first read through the six chapters of Ephesians and see which chapter or which portion they should speak. If they do not have enough burden, then they should go and read the footnotes and the *Life-study of the New Testament* from which they could surely find a portion or two which are fitting. If they can find five or six pages of material, that would be sufficient.

It is best to announce at the Lord's table what will be read the next Lord's Day and to ask the saints to bring the Life-studies. However, it is not enough to merely read. You have to speak while reading, but do not speak too much; it is sufficient just to point out a few things. Not only one person, but everyone can read and point out certain points. First read a few verses, then pray-read them, and then read a few paragraphs of explanation. In this way I believe that everyone will be satisfied. There are fifty-two weeks in a year, and every week we could have two such meetings, so altogether there would be one hundred and four meetings a year. In this way the saints would be able to hear the Lord's words of life and to receive nourishment from them.

Almost everywhere in the world there is the custom of resting from work on the Lord's Day; everyone has a day of vacation and rest. Therefore, we have to utilize the Lord's Day morning to diligently work on the truth, speak the truth, and teach the truth. If possible, on the Lord's Day morning we should have not only one kind of meeting, but three or four kinds of meetings at the same time—one that is not too deep, another one that is little deeper, and still another that is even deeper. We must have all kinds of meetings. At present we are still in the process of research, and I hope that after the changing of the system we could strictly put these things into practice so that the saints may receive the teaching. In this way, after three to five years the saints among us will have made great progress in knowing, speaking, and explaining the truth. Everyone will be able to speak for God, speaking every day and speaking everywhere, in season and out of season; they will be able to speak at any time and in any place.

Today the whole world is in a spiritual drought; every place is lacking the word of God and the truth of God. If we depend only on the preachers to speak and minister the word, the word will be very limited and very restricted. What we need today is for all the saints to speak the word of God. If we all speak, in the end the word of God will grow and multiply greatly and will also become strong (Acts 6:7; 12:24; 19:20).

CHAPTER FOUR

THE CHRISTIAN MEETING
BEING A MATTER OF SPEAKING

The purpose of the Christian meeting is to prophesy, to speak. This is just like saying that the purpose of a ball team is to play ball; the ball is the focus of a ball team. When a ball team comes together, it does so to play ball. If there is no ball, there is no reason to have a ball team. Hence, we have to see that the Christian meeting is not a so-called worship service but a gathering for all to prophesy, to speak Christ.

Sixty years ago when we were raised up by the Lord in China, we were all young people. Today we are very happy because we see that in the church there are also numerous young people. This encourages us very much. If in a worldly profession there is no younger generation, then that profession has no future. Similarly, the rise or fall of a family depends on the next generation. No matter how able and capable the older generations—the grandparents and the parents—of a family are, if there are no heirs to continue the family line, then the family will not have any future.

We thank the Lord that in the church there are many older saints, because without them the church would not have any descendants. Therefore, we should not be ungrateful toward the older saints. Nonetheless, it is very good that we have many young people in the church. When I see these young people, I feel like I am a coach teaching these young ones how to play ball. We Christians are a ball team, and our meeting is a ball game. Even when we are not competing, we are still practicing. The ball is the word, the ball game is our meeting, and our ball playing is our speaking.

To play ball well, one must play skillfully and accurately.

Likewise, to speak in the meetings we have to be able to speak the word clearly. In the past we came to the meetings without bringing the "ball." Instead, everyone came empty-handed, coming only to "go to church." However, in our "going to church" there was no prophesying, no speaking. The Christian meeting is not for "going to church" but for speaking, for prophesying. Traditional Christianity has been deceived and has been utilized by Satan to completely discard the treasure of our heritage—the Bible, the speaking of God. We have to recover this. We must see that the purpose of the Christian meeting is speaking. When Christians meet together, there should be speaking.

NOT WORSHIPPING DUMB IDOLS
BUT SPEAKING IN GOD'S NAME

The Christian meeting is not for the worshipping of dumb idols (1 Cor. 12:2). If the Christian meeting is for "going to church," then it is the worshipping of dumb idols. Before I was twenty years old, I was saved and delivered out of the worldly system; at that time I began to love the Lord and to study the Bible diligently. Now it has been over half a century, and I have studied the Bible quite thoroughly. Besides reading the Bible, I have also read and studied in depth the history of the church, biographies of famous people throughout the generations, and the orthodox teachings. From my readings I saw the subtlety of Satan, particularly in the Middle Ages, when European architecture was altogether focused on building cathedrals. Nearly all the European-style cathedrals, as well as the cathedrals from earlier time periods, have a towering outward appearance, stained-glass windows, and a dark interior. The purpose of this is to produce a psychological effect on people so that once they step into the building, they are struck with awe and dare not make a sound. All they can do is just find a seat and then sit down and begin to have the "worship service." In doing so, they are worshipping dumb idols.

The European architecture in those days was the result of much study; it was altogether for the purpose of accommodating man's psychological desire to "go to church." This shows us that it was the work of the devil. The devil's activities are very much involved in many architectural structures. For instance, when people go into a Chinese temple, not only do the things inside the temple arouse fear in them but even walking into the temple gives them a gloomy feeling. The stratagem of the enemy is to make the Christian meeting place exactly like a temple for idols, causing the Christian meeting to become a dumb service of one man speaking and all the rest listening.

I hope that we all can see the light, so that we can see the Lord's desire, Satan's strategy, and the degradation of the church. Christianity has fallen into such a pitiful condition that the Lord has no position and no freedom to speak there. All the chapels and cathedrals, whether big or small, have been constructed in a way that causes people to remain silent. Consequently, the believers not only do not know how to preach the word, they do not even know how to pray and do not dare to pray. This exposes the subtlety of Satan in annulling the functioning of the children of God, even to the extent that it is impossible for the Body of Christ to exist. We know that the existence of the Body depends on the functioning of all the members together; if the members of our physical body do not function, there is no way for our body to exist.

We need the Lord's mercy for this light to shine brighter and brighter among us that we may see that attending the meeting is not "going to church" for the worship of dumb idols. When Paul wrote 1 Corinthians chapters twelve through fourteen, he inserted chapter thirteen to speak about love. The preceding and succeeding chapters—chapters twelve and fourteen—are the focus of this section, showing us that the Christian meeting is not for "going to church." Rather, the Christian meeting is for speaking, for everyone to speak the word of God, for everyone to "play ball." In chapter twelve Paul mentioned a total of nine items concerning the manifestation of the Spirit in the believers. This is not to say that there are only nine items of the manifestation of the Spirit; rather, these nine items were listed as an illustration. The most important items of the manifestation of the Spirit in us are the first two mentioned by Paul: first, a word of wisdom, and second, a word of knowledge (v. 8). Therefore, the "ball" we use is a "wisdom ball" and also a "knowledge ball." Ordinarily, the ball we play with is very simple, but the ball we use in the church meeting is not so simple—it is a "wisdom ball" and also a "knowledge ball."

If there is no speaking in the Christian meeting, then it is equivalent to playing ball without the ball. Some of the believers may say the reason they do not speak is not that they do not want to speak but that they do not know what to speak. After visiting the churches in various localities, we received a general impression that in the church meetings there is a shortage of the word and a lack of speaking. Even the singing is limited to a few hymns. It seems that besides these few, there are no other hymns. The same is true in the matter of praying. You can predict who will pray, because it is always the same five or six persons. It seems that these ones form a prayer group representing everyone else. After these few pray, it is almost time to dismiss the meeting. The rest of the attendants are just the supporting cast.

Many years ago a number of our co-workers felt that it was very hard to be a co-worker, because in addition to giving a message every Lord's Day, they also had to give a message in the middle of the week for fifty-two weeks a year. Preparing to give a message was not at all easy; rather, it was laborious. After delivering the message on the Lord's Day morning, they may have felt somewhat relieved, but then soon it was Wednesday, and they had to consider what they would speak on Thursday. After speaking on Thursday, they again breathed a little easier, but after Friday, Saturday soon arrived and the need for the Lord's Day message was pressing hard on them again. Thus, week after week it was the same cycle. The co-workers all felt the hardship because they had nothing to speak, they had no ball to play with. This was the general situation in those days.

In the past when Brother Nee was leading us, he clearly said that we should not do any work in the way of one person doing everything, but we should do it in coordination with other brothers. He charged us to keep this principle faithfully, and according to his instruction we tried to do things, not in the way of one person doing everything but in the way of coordination with others. However, the fact that everyone was responsible for the work meant that no one was responsible. For instance, suppose four of us responsible brothers sit together in the meeting. You look at me, and I look at you, until finally one of us cannot bear it anymore, so he selects a hymn for everyone to sing. Such a situation showed us that we did not have a "ball" to play with.

For this reason, starting from 1974, I was determined to release the riches of the divine revelation in the Lord's word; in this way we would have "balls" for us to use. Now we have so many "balls" that we do not know how to choose from them. This one looks good, and the other is not bad either. This may be likened to going to a department store. Due to the great variety of merchandise, we are simply confused and do not know which item we should buy. Therefore, there are salespersons who are trained to know how to show people only a few selected items. Maybe they would introduce you to only one item or perhaps five or ten items, but they would not bring out all the items.

Likewise, today the "balls" are all here. The *Life-study of the New Testament* alone contains more than 1,200 topics, and if we count the pages, there are more than ten thousand pages. Within these pages, the riches we can use, the "balls" we can use for playing, are difficult to count, and it is hard for us to know how to select from them. Therefore, today the problem is not that there are no "balls"; rather, the problem is that we do not know how to select a "ball," nor do we know how to use it. Sometimes people bring a large number of "balls" into the meeting. Some end up playing in this direction and others in another direction. The result is great confusion. Therefore, the problem is not only that there are too many "balls" and that we do not know how to select a "ball"; the problem is also that what we have selected might not be fitting, and even when it is suitable, we might not know how to use it. This is our difficulty.

Therefore, within some of the saints there is a voice saying, "Let us go back to holding worship services! The way of everyone speaking is too hard; let us go back to the way of one person speaking and the rest listening." Thus, some would choose the easy way and go back to train preachers and then assign them to preach. They would say, "After all, this is also doing the work of the Lord." However, if this becomes the case, how will the Lord have a way to go on? Will the word of the Lord still be propagated and prevailing? No, the Lord will have no way to go on and propagate. If we look at the various Christian organizations, we can see that they all have a long history, yet they do not have much increase, nor do they allow the Lord to have a way to go on.

How we hope that every one of us would have a ball in our hands and know how to use it, and that we all would play using the same ball. This is our goal, and this is what the Bible teaches us. In 1 Corinthians 12 Paul said that we are not worshipping dumb idols, but we are speaking in the Spirit of God (vv. 2-3). When we come to the meeting, we must be in the Spirit of God, because when we are in the Spirit of God we cannot and will not be dumb. When we speak, we are in the Spirit of God.

The young people do not dare to speak in the meeting primarily because they are shy. They feel that they are the younger generation, so they are nervous and scared and wait for the older ones to open their mouths first. In this way they naturally become dumb, trying to worship God without exercising their spirit. Over a long period of time, this becomes their habit. This is not the proper condition. When the young people come to a meeting, they have to take the initiative to exercise their spirit and say, "Hallelujah! Praise the Lord!" Then they should release their spirit and pray, "O Lord Jesus! We love You." When you open your mouth in this way, you will breathe freely, and your spirit will be released.

In the universe there are fixed laws in God's creation and in His redemption. Do not think that to call "O Lord Jesus" is an easy matter. If we were to ask an unsaved person to call "O Lord Jesus," that would be a very difficult matter. Even if you held him by his throat to force him to say it, he might not be able to say it because Satan is there. When we talk to people about Chinese philosophers such as Confucius and Wang Yang-ming, they feel glorious and honored. But when we talk to them about the Lord Jesus, they feel ashamed and oppose us. This is because Satan, the devil, is still walking about, seeking someone to devour (1 Pet. 5:8). This is why the gospel is a battle.

The fact that we are able to spontaneously call "O Lord Jesus" is a strong proof that we have been saved, that we have been delivered out of the power of Satan, and that we are now in spirit. The more Christians call "O Lord Jesus," the better. Stanza 1 of *Hymns,* #208 says, "O Jesus,...I say...Thy sacred name / A thousand times a day." The writer of this hymn said that he says the Lord's name a thousand times a day. Actually a thousand times is still not enough. This is just like our breathing—it is hard to count the number of times we breathe daily. We breathe continuously; we breathe without ceasing. Paul told the Corinthians that whenever they meet, instead of worshipping the dumb idols, they should speak in the Holy Spirit. "No one speaking in the Spirit of God says, Jesus is accursed; and no one can say, Jesus is Lord! except in the Holy Spirit" (1 Cor. 12:3).

Whenever we meet, we are not worshipping the idols, so we should not be dumb; rather, we are breathing a living Lord, so we all must speak for the Lord. *Hymns,* #864 is on exhibiting Christ. Although exhibiting Christ is good, it might be a dumb exhibition. It would be good if we changed *exhibiting Christ* to *speaking Christ,* because in speaking Christ we surely cannot be dumb. In the meetings, not only do we exhibit Christ, but even the more we speak Christ.

In our natural concept we always feel that our own testimony is too common and too shallow and that it is not worth the trouble to speak and testify about it. However, we must see that to speak in the meeting is not a question of whether or not we ought to testify; rather, it is a question of whether or not we ought to breathe. For instance, although I am an older brother, I may come into the meeting filled with the Spirit and say, "Hallelujah! I am saved. While I was still a student, one day the Lord Jesus met me, and I did not want the world any longer; the Lord captured me." This kind of testimony is living and fresh. Therefore, do not think that it is useless to give an old testimony. We can turn an old testimony into a new testimony; it all depends on whether or not our spirit is living. As long as our spirit is living, even if we speak just a few sentences in the meeting, the congregation will sense the freshness and be supplied. Therefore, the Christian meeting is for speaking.

THE TWO MOST IMPORTANT ITEMS
OF THE MANIFESTATION OF THE SPIRIT
IN THE BELIEVERS BEING THE WORD OF WISDOM
AND THE WORD OF KNOWLEDGE

The two most important items of the manifestation of the Spirit in the believers are the word of wisdom and the word of knowledge. Those who are engaged in the Pentecostal movement often hold on to 1 Corinthians and refuse to let go. They have not seen, however, that although 1 Corinthians talks about the spiritual gifts, it actually depreciates their value to almost nothing. Those in Pentecostalism uplift the spiritual gifts to the highest place. Yet 1 Corinthians shows us that among the nine items of the manifestation of the Spirit, the two most important ones are the word of wisdom and the word of knowledge, and the two least important ones are the speaking in tongues and interpretation of tongues (12:8, 10).

The Scriptures clearly show us that the first two items of the manifestation of the Spirit in the believers are the word of wisdom and the word of knowledge. Those in the Pentecostal movement absolutely do not have these; they have neither the word of wisdom nor the word or knowledge. Our meetings, however, are filled with the word of wisdom and the word of knowledge. After I started the work in America, I released several hundred messages during a period of only two or three years, and every message was a word of wisdom and also a word of knowledge. Today those who are engaged in the Pentecostal movement are unceasingly speaking in tongues and interpreting the tongues. In Paul's time, the speaking in tongues and interpretation of tongues were genuine; however, most of today's speaking in tongues and interpretation of tongues are false. The tongue-speaking today is merely the sound of the tongue. The tongues spoken in the New Testament were words which could be understood by people; if they were not understandable, Paul would not have talked about interpretation of tongues. If tongues are spoken, they must be interpreted; if what is spoken cannot be interpreted, then it is not the tongue-speaking referred to in the Scriptures.

According to research it was discovered that those who speak in tongues are mostly middle-aged women, yet those who interpret tongues are mostly men. The contents of the interpretations are all about the same; most of them say, "My people, the time is short; I am coming. Be watchful and pray. The gospel must be preached to the whole earth." Furthermore, although different languages are used, such as Chinese and English, their intonations are the same, and the phrases are almost identical. A later research found out that in America there is a school for prophesying which specializes in teaching people these techniques.

In the New Testament Paul encouraged every one of us to prophesy, to speak (1 Cor. 14:31). This is not to speak the so-called tongues, but to speak the word of wisdom and the word of knowledge. First Corinthians 12:8 says, "For to one through the Spirit a word of wisdom is given, and to another a word of knowledge, according to the same Spirit." The Recovery Version of the New Testament has a footnote on that verse, which says, "According to the context of this book, the word of wisdom is the word concerning Christ as the deeper things of God, predestined by God to be our portion (1:24, 30; 2:6-10). The word of knowledge is the word that imparts a general knowledge of things concerning God and the Lord (8:1-7). The word of wisdom is mainly out of our spirit through revelation; the word of knowledge is mainly out of our understanding through teaching. The former is deeper than the latter. However, both of these, not speaking in tongues nor any other miraculous gift, are listed as the first gifts and the topmost manifestation of the Spirit because both are the most profitable ministries, or services, for the edification of the saints and the building up of the church to carry out God's operation" (note 1). This really shows us that our meeting is a matter of speaking, which consists mainly of two kinds of words: the word of wisdom and the word of knowledge. These two kinds of words require our labor. The word of wisdom concerns the deep things of Christ, and the word of knowledge concerns the general knowledge of God and of Christ. This requires us to labor on the Word of God, spending more time to study, to learn, to compare, and to know. Then, either the Holy Spirit will give us revelation in our spirit for us to have the word of wisdom, or He will give us teaching in our mind for us to have the word of knowledge. The words we speak in the meetings, that is, the "balls" we use, are of these two kinds: one is the word of wisdom, and the other is the word of knowledge.

THE CONTENTS OF THE BELIEVERS' MEETINGS BEING PSALMS, TEACHINGS, AND REVELATIONS

First Corinthians 14:26 says, "What then, brothers? Whenever you come together...." The coming together here refers not to a small meeting, such as a group meeting, but to the big meetings of the church, because verse 23 says, "If therefore the whole church comes together in one place...." Therefore, the coming together mentioned in verse 26 should refer to the big meetings of the whole church gathered together. Whenever the saints come together and meet in this way, "each one has a psalm, has a teaching, has a revelation, has a tongue, has an interpretation. Let all things be done for building up." This is the only verse in the New Testament which tells us what to do when we meet. Whenever the whole church comes together, each one should have this or have that. *Each one* does not mean just one person but every person.

In verse 26 the word *has* is used five times. Paul tells us that in the meeting each one has a psalm, has a teaching, has a revelation, has a tongue, or has an interpretation. The last two items, a tongue and an interpretation, are easy to understand. The first three items are a psalm, a teaching, and a revelation; among these three, a teaching and a revelation are matters of speaking. Concerning the word *has,* the Recovery Version of the New Testament has a note which says, *"Has,* occurring five times in this verse, is a widely used Greek word, a word with many meanings, of which the following three are the main ones: (1) *to hold, to possess, to keep (a certain thing);* (2) *to have (a certain thing) for enjoyment;* (3) *to have the means or power to do a certain thing.* The first two meanings should be applied to the first three of the five items listed in this verse, and the third to the last two—a tongue and an interpretation of a tongue" (note 1).

The first item mentioned is a psalm, which is for praising the Lord. If we read again Ephesians 5 and Colossians 3, we will see that these two chapters tell us that psalms are not so much for singing as they are for speaking to one another (Eph. 5:19; Col. 3:16). Of course, psalms are for singing; however, according to the New Testament, psalms are even more for speaking to one another. Speaking to one another with psalms and hymns is more powerful and more inspiring. Therefore, not only do we need to sing the hymns, but even more we should speak the hymns. We need to cultivate this habit.

We should speak not only ordinary words but also poems and hymns. Poems and songs are the cream of the human language. If a language has not reached a stage of maturity, it cannot produce poems and songs, which are very powerful for the expression of feelings. Many of the hymns in our hymnal are worth speaking to one another. For example, *Hymns,* #864 is very suitable for singing and speaking to one another. Stanza 1 and the chorus say, "Whene'er we meet with Christ endued, / The surplus of His plenitude / We offer unto God as food, / And thus exhibit Christ. / Let us exhibit Christ, / Let us exhibit Christ; / We'll bring His surplus to the church / And thus exhibit Christ." We can compare whether the taste is richer by singing or by speaking the hymn. Both ways are very meaningful.

Not only can we practice singing and speaking to one another while we are in the meetings, but when we go back to our homes and even while we are still on the way, we can also practice this. We all know that in playing basketball, there is not just one way to pass the ball but many ways. For instance, one can pass the ball through the air, or he can pass the ball by bouncing it on the ground. In like manner, we should not be too rigid in our singing of hymns. Sometimes once a hymn has been selected, we may sing through the whole hymn stanza by stanza. Sometimes singing to one another is very meaningful also. Other times we can alternately sing and speak. After singing the first stanza, we speak the second stanza, then we sing the third stanza and speak the fourth stanza; we do this alternately until we get to the last stanza. Afterward, we may come back to the first stanza and sing it again. We can practice different ways until we become skillful, just as basketball players can pass the ball on the court in various ways.

After singing and speaking, speaking and singing a hymn, we still need more speaking. Whenever we meet, we mainly want to bring Christ with us and to minister Christ to others. However, if we want to bring Christ to the meeting, we must first have Christ. Therefore, we still need a good message; then the meeting can be rich. God has given us two gifts: the Spirit and the Word. Today the Spirit is within us while the Word is in our hands. Moreover, many portions of the Word have become hymns and songs. For example, *Hymns,* #864 is a product of the exposition of the truth to the fullest extent. In the chorus, "Let us exhibit Christ" is a picture of how the children of Israel in the Old Testament brought the riches from their field to Jerusalem for exhibition during their feasts. Therefore, in the New Testament when Christians meet together, they should bring the riches of Christ to exhibit them together.

This indicates that when we come to the church meeting, we should have something of the Lord to share with others, whether a psalm to praise the Lord, a teaching (of the teacher) to minister the riches of Christ to edify and nourish others, a revelation of the prophet (1 Cor. 14:30) to give visions of God's eternal purpose concerning Christ as God's mystery and the church as Christ's mystery, a tongue for a sign to the unbelievers (v. 22) that they may know and accept Christ, or an interpretation to make a tongue concerning Christ and His Body understandable. The tongue-speaking here is not the so-called sound of the tongue and prophesying as practiced by the Pentecostal people. What Paul speaks about here, whether a teaching, a revelation, a tongue, or an interpretation, all ought to be the speaking of Christ. Some speak in the way of teaching, some speak in the way of revelation, some use the way of tongue-speaking, and some speak by the interpretation of tongues. No matter how one speaks, the content must be Christ. According to the whole book of 1 Corinthians, its general subject is Christ being the wisdom to us from God, as righteousness, sanctification, and redemption. He is our all in all.

Before coming to the meeting we should prepare ourselves for the meeting with such things from the Lord and of the Lord, either through our experiences of Him or through our enjoyment of His word and fellowship with Him in prayer. After coming into the meeting, we need not wait, and should not wait, for inspiration; we should exercise our spirit and use our trained mind to function in presenting what we have prepared to the Lord for His glory and satisfaction and to the attendants for their benefit—their enlightenment, nourishment, and building up.

This is like the Feast of Tabernacles in ancient times. The children of Israel brought the produce of the good land, which they had reaped from their labor on the land, to the feast and offered it to the Lord for His enjoyment and for their mutual participation in fellowship with the Lord and with one another. We must labor on Christ, our good land, that we may reap some produce of His riches to bring to the church meeting and offer. Thus, the meeting will be an exhibition of Christ in His riches and will be a mutual enjoyment of Christ shared by all the attendants before God and with God for the building up of the saints and the church.

THE MOST PROFITABLE ACTIVITY
IN THE CHURCH MEETING BEING PROPHESYING

The most profitable activity in the church meeting is not the performing of miracles, nor healing, nor the casting out of demons, nor the speaking in tongues, nor the interpreting of tongues. The most profitable activity is prophesying (vv. 23-25).

EVERY BELIEVER BEING ABLE TO PROPHESY
ONE BY ONE

First Corinthians 14:31 says, "For you can all prophesy one by one that all may learn and all may be encouraged." Anyone who is saved can prophesy.

THE GIFT THE BELIEVERS NEED TO DESIRE MOST
BEING THE PROPHESYING
FOR THE BUILDING UP OF THE CHURCH

The gift the believers need to desire most is the prophesying for the building up of the church. The conclusion of Paul's speaking from 1 Corinthians chapters twelve through fourteen is that the gift the believers need to desire most is the speaking for the Lord, the prophesying as prophets. The one gift that benefits others the most is also prophesying (14:1, 3, 4b). The Lord not only gives us the permission and the position; He also gives us the ability so that we "can all prophesy one by one" (v. 31). Therefore, we must see that as those who have been begotten of God, we have the position and the ability to prophesy.

THE ELDERS NEEDING TO BE APT TO TEACH
AND TO LABOR ON GOD'S WORD
AND THE BELIEVERS NEEDING TO BE FAITHFUL
IN LEARNING TO TEACH OTHERS

Every one of the saints should speak for the Lord by prophesying, but the elders need to take the lead in speaking. If the elders do not speak in the meetings, it will be hard for the saints to open their mouths. Hence, a basic qualification of an elder is that he must be apt to teach (1 Tim. 3:2; 5:17; 2 Tim. 2:2). The phrase *apt to* has the notion of "being accustomed to," "having the habit of," or "being used to." Hence, the elders needing to be apt to teach means that they should not only be well able to speak the Lord's word but also be accustomed to, and have the habit of, speaking the Lord's word. In this way it will be easy for the saints to follow and form a habit so that once they come to the meeting, they are also apt to speak and are used to speaking.

On the other hand, do not occupy too much time when you speak. This is similar to playing basketball. When the ball comes to your hands, you have to pass it on quickly so that ultimately the ball can go into the basket. Therefore, when you speak in the meeting, do not speak too long nor speak too many times; after speaking once, you should wait and let others speak. We should always remember that each of us is just a member of the Body and that there are still many other saints in the meeting. Therefore, we must learn to yield to them the opportunity.

First Timothy 5:17 says that the elders must labor in word and teaching. *Labor* here is a particular word. In Greek it denotes not the effort exerted in doing a general work but the strenuous effort exerted for "building up a business from scratch"; it does not mean to work but to spend great effort on the Word of God. There is a meaningful cartoon which is an appropriate picture of laboring, depicting how hard the children in Taiwan study. In the picture a boy is studying with the mother feeding him, the father cooling him with a fan, and the younger brother taking his shoes off for him. Many of us know that the education in Taiwan is widespread, yet its standard is higher than most other countries. This is due to the laboring of Taiwan's children in their education with the help of their parents and siblings.

Therefore, the elders should not be at ease; they must take great pains to study the Bible, and their families must wait on them and support them. Every one of the elders must devote himself to labor on the Word of God. This is what I do myself; I labor daily on the Lord's word. Every month I have to publish sixteen or seventeen Life-study messages, totaling nearly two hundred pages. Even when I have to travel far away from home, I still do not delay the work; I always have to spend a few days hurrying day and night. I might not be as smart as you are, but I know one thing—I am more diligent than you. Therefore, the New Testament has been thoroughly digested within me from early on, and I can even say that it has been constituted into me. Now, I can use the ball in every possible way. I am quite confident in passing the ball, receiving the ball, and shooting the ball.

Therefore, I hope that the elders would not be too comfortable or at ease; you have to spend more effort and time on the Lord's word. Furthermore, the elders' family members must give them a great deal of help so that they may wholeheartedly enter into the Lord's word. The elders must all labor on the Lord's word. Over thirty years ago when I went to the Philippines, the Chinese in Southeast Asia were successful in every profession. In whatever line of business or profession they chose, the overseas Chinese were always at the top because they were diligent, they labored hard, and they did real work. However, the amazing thing was that there was only one profession that did not produce topnotch people, and that was the profession of preaching the word. Even the preachers who went to Southeast Asia did not work hard. Therefore, I hope that the elders see this point clearly. When you lead the church, you must be like the successful Chinese in Southeast Asia who have a spirit that is unbeatable in diligence, laboring, and endeavoring.

By the mercy of the Lord, I have been a miner who has opened the mouth of the gold mine of the twenty-seven books of the New Testament. However, you yourself must dig out the gold within the mine. If all of us would do this, then in the Lord's recovery we would be rich in the word, and the churches in all the localities would also flourish. What we should do by the grace of the Lord is bring people into the Lord's word and not into our teachings. What we should do is bring all the saints into the riches of the twenty-seven books of the New Testament. This requires us to enter into this together.

Therefore, the elders still have to spend their effort and take the lead in this matter so that the younger generation can follow and also enter in. In this way in five or ten years, the situations in the various churches surely will be different and will draw the respect of people from deep within. When people come into our midst, listening to the prayers of the young people and the sharing of the older saints, and observing the labor of the elders, they surely will feel that this family is rich, that it is a learned family with a great future.

We must labor on the Lord's word so that when we speak in the meeting, we would speak the word of wisdom and the word of knowledge instead of the loose words, light words, and meaningless tongues. What the saints need is the proper word—the word of wisdom and the word of knowledge.

As a result, everyone who is faithful in the Lord's word will be able to go forth to speak and teach others. Everyone will be a prophet, and everyone will become an apostle. As they go forth and preach, they will bring some people to be saved and cause some to rise up and love the Lord; in this way they will establish some churches. These are the things done by the teachers, prophets, and apostles. This is a work that glorifies the Lord. We absolutely believe that in these last days the Lord will greatly expand this work.

Chapter Five

THE WAY TO SPEAK FOR GOD
IN VARIOUS KINDS OF MEETINGS

To say that the purpose of the Christian meeting is for speaking is altogether against traditional Christianity. According to traditional Christianity, the Christian meeting is called *tso-li-pai* in Chinese, which literally means "doing a worship." Such an expression, which was probably coined by the Western missionaries who did not know Chinese adequately, is puzzling to the Chinese people. The Chinese have expressions such as *tso-fan* (prepare a meal), *tso-i-fu* (make a dress), *tso-chia-shih* (do housework), *tso-kung-k'e* (do homework), *tso-hsueh-wen* (learn knowledge), *tso-cho-tzu* (make a table), and *tso-i-tzu* (make a chair). All these expressions are understandable. However, to say *tso-li-pai*—"doing a worship" or "making a worship"—is difficult to understand.

From the Bible we see that the way Christians meet is a matter of immense importance. Unfortunately, due to the degradation of the church, Christians have gradually deviated from taking the proper way in many important matters, and the most important of them all is the matter of meeting. Therefore, we want to investigate the history of Christian, or church, meetings.

THE CHURCH LIFE STARTED
BY THE FIRST GROUP OF CHRISTIANS

The last part of Acts chapter two shows us that on the day of Pentecost three thousand were saved and baptized into the name of the Lord (v. 41), and then these ones immediately began to meet together. The way they met was clearly recorded in the second chapter of Acts. Acts 2:46 says, "And day by day, continuing steadfastly with one accord in the temple and breaking bread from house to house, they partook of their food with exultation and simplicity of heart." The Greek words translated *from house to house* mean "in every home." Those who know a little Greek know that this expression *from house to house* is quite fitting. It indicates that the early believers met together not only in the temple but also in their homes, from house to house.

In chapter five, the last verse says, "And every day, in the temple and from house to house, they did not cease teaching and announcing the gospel of Jesus as the Christ" (v. 42). The early believers did two things. The first thing they did was teach people. We believe that what they taught was surely based on the truths they heard from Peter and John, and they taught from house to house. The second thing they did was announce the gospel of Jesus as the Christ. These were the two things they did. On the one hand, they taught the truths, and on the other hand, they announced the gospel; furthermore, they did these things from house to house.

This verse also shows us that at Pentecost, when the Christians began to meet, their meetings were of two kinds. On the one hand, they had meetings in the temple; these were big meetings. On the other hand, they had meetings in the homes, from house to house; these were small meetings. However, we must realize one thing. The actions of the believers on the day of Pentecost were altogether the actions of the Holy Spirit who was poured out upon them. On the day of Pentecost, the outpouring of the Holy Spirit was particularly intense, and the atmosphere of the presence of the Holy Spirit was especially strong; that was a great move of the Holy Spirit. After hearing the gospel, many were pricked in their heart, and asked Peter, "What should we do?" Peter answered, "Repent and each one of you be baptized upon the name of Jesus Christ for the forgiveness of your sins" (2:37-38). Thus, they all repented and were baptized. After they were baptized, they began to have big meetings in the temple and also small meetings from house to house. From this we cannot help acknowledging that their actions were absolutely of the Holy Spirit and were the move of the Holy

Spirit, because never in the history of the Jewish people had there been such a thing as meeting from house to house.

This way of meeting initiated by the first group of Christians for their church life on the day of Pentecost was a creation and a masterpiece of the Holy Spirit and was led and ordained by the Holy Spirit. This way of meeting created by the Holy Spirit was of two aspects. On the one hand, there were the big meetings in the temple, and on the other hand, there were the small meetings from house to house. If we read this portion of the Word in a thorough manner, we will see that this was proper. The big meetings were held in the temple so that people could be brought in order to gain them. In order to gain the Jewish people, the big meetings in the temple were necessary. This is similar to our practice today. We preach the gospel in the gospel meetings to lead people to salvation. After they have been baptized, we turn them over to the small meetings held from house to house. In these small meetings held from house to house, the newly saved ones can function comfortably, be preserved, and learn to take care of others.

The three thousand began to meet from house to house no later than the second day after their baptism. Since they had only heard one or two messages before they began to meet from house to house, they could not have spoken in the meetings according to the traditional way of the Jews. What they spoke must have been according to what they had heard from Peter. Although the gospel message Peter gave on that day contained quotations from only the Old Testament, those quotations were all related to Christ. In Acts 2 Peter spoke about Christ's death and resurrection based on the prophecies in the Old Testament concerning Christ (vv. 25-36). I believe that after the three thousand were saved, what they spoke in their meetings from house to house was concerning these matters.

In the initial stage of the church, the first group of three thousand, after being saved and baptized, began to have small group meetings from house to house. If these three thousand people had been divided into groups of six, they would have formed five hundred groups. Acts 2:42 is actually a little window through which we can see a great number of things.

First of all, in the matter of dividing into groups, there probably was not enough time for Peter or the one hundred and twenty saints to have made arrangements for the five hundred groups and to tell them what they should do. Nor was there enough time for them to have examined the three thousand people in order to determine whose homes were suitable for group meetings and whose homes were not nor to determine who was sufficiently qualified and who was not. After the three thousand had been saved, Peter probably did not know what to do with them, and even if the one hundred and twenty saints had all become his helpers, there still would not have been enough time for them to fully know all the newly saved ones. There was no way any arrangement or assignment concerning their meeting together could have been made; hence, it must have been the work of the Holy Spirit.

The record in the Bible tells us that after their baptism the early believers began to meet day by day in the temple and in their homes, from house to house. This shows us that this move was not initiated by Peter; it originated altogether from the Holy Spirit. The Holy Spirit moved within the newly saved ones, causing them to realize that after being baptized, they could no longer behave as Jews and to realize that since they had all received the Lord Jesus and were baptized, they should meet in their own homes. Therefore, they began to meet together. It was a very spontaneous thing. No one was taking the lead; rather, it was the Holy Spirit Himself who led them.

Concerning the way to meet, last year in Taiwan the Lord showed us a clear revelation. Even among us, the elements of traditional Christianity still have not been completely purged out, just like a stream of water contaminated with sulfur. This is why we felt that we had to change the system in order to reverse our past habits. However, we realized that we cannot get rid of the big meetings, and neither can we be without the small meetings. Neither one can be dispensed with. This is similar to the fact that a 747 airplane cannot fly by relying merely on a single wing, a bird cannot fly by depending on only one wing, and even a man cannot walk with just one leg. This is why God created man with two legs and birds with two wings, and, in accordance with God's principle, why men make airplanes with a right wing and a left wing. The traditional way of meeting as Christians is like flying with one wing only. In the big meeting every Lord's Day, only one person speaks and the rest just listen; everyone merely attends a worship service. Consequently, there is no way to go on. The Bible reveals that in addition to the big meetings in the temple, there must be the small meetings from house to house, the group gatherings. This is what we have to see.

We are very clear that man can never create or originate anything; man can only produce something by first studying and learning about it. However, on the day of Pentecost the Holy Spirit truly created a new thing. When God created the heavens and the earth with all the things, He did not need to research or to improve His creation later; whatever He created was the best. No one can improve God's creation, whether it is the heavens and the earth created by God or the features of man. Today in constructing a tall building or in paving a road, we need an architect to make designs and changes. Yet no one can alter or re-create the heavens and the earth, nor can anyone alter man's face. If the nose of a man were moved and placed on top of his eyes or the lips were placed upon the eyebrows, would that be functional? If the ears were changed so that one ear was placed in front and the other at the back, or if the shoulders were to be of different heights, would that be practical? What God has created cannot be altered or improved by man. Therefore, for the three thousand who were saved on the day of Pentecost to have small group meetings from house to house was the creation of the Holy Spirit, and that was the best way.

EVERYONE TAKING THE LEAD
IN THE SMALL GROUP MEETING

In the church life we have seen that many brothers want to be the head. This is true in both the West and in the East. However, in Matthew 20 the Lord Jesus told the disciples, "Whoever wants to become great among you shall be your servant, and whoever wants to be first among you shall be your slave" (vv. 26b-27). Hence, every elder must realize that he is not the head but a slave.

Twenty or thirty years ago in Taiwan, there were some sisters who loved the Lord very much. They had hoped to be the leading sisters of some home meetings, ones who were called "home responsible ones" at that time. Some among them were very spiritual, but due to certain improper family situations, they were not assigned to be responsible ones. Greatly disappointed, these sisters were not able to eat well and sleep well for a few weeks, and their meeting life became abnormal. It took several weeks of becoming ill or encountering some situations before they came back to the meetings. There have been many such stories.

Ever since the meetings in Taiwan went through the change in the system last year, the emphasis has no longer been on the big meetings. Rather, like two wings, the big meetings and the small meetings have been balanced. When the group meetings were first established, we fellowshipped with the saints, saying that henceforth there would be no leading ones in the group meetings. Everybody was surprised upon hearing this, wondering how they could have a meeting without someone taking the lead. If no one takes the lead, then that means everyone is a leader and everyone can lead. However, whoever takes the lead is not humanly appointed but is under the leading of the Holy Spirit.

To be more cautious, we studied and considered the Scriptures anew concerning these matters. We saw that firstly, when the Lord Jesus was on the earth, He Himself appointed twelve apostles, but He did not establish a leader among them. Secondly, after the day of Pentecost when the number of disciples had multiplied and the practical affairs of the church had increased, the twelve apostles called together the disciples and told them, "It is not fitting for us to forsake the word of God and serve tables. But brothers, look for seven well-attested men from among you, full of the Spirit and of wisdom, whom we will appoint over this need" (Acts 6:2b-3). From this portion of the Bible we do not see the apostles selecting one out of the seven to be the "head deacon." According to the human concept, there ought to be a leader, but there is no record in the Bible of such a thing.

Thirdly, going further, we saw that in 1 Timothy Paul charged the elders concerning many things, saying that the elders should be this and that. Nonetheless, in the end he did not ask the elders to choose one among themselves to be the "head elder." From these three portions, we clearly see, and can boldly say, that in the Bible there is neither a "head apostle," a "head elder," nor a "head deacon." We cannot even find an example of someone being designated as the one who assembles the apostles, who calls the elders together, or who gathers the deacons.

Our experience tells us that once there is an arrangement, there will be damage. Someone may become not only the head elder but may even become the "elder-emperor." This is the danger of someone becoming the head. Due to these difficulties, the church has suffered no small injuries and wounds over the past thirty years. Therefore, in changing the system this time, we declared that we would have the small groups, but we would not have someone designated to take the lead because everyone should be a leading one.

THE ORIGIN AND BACKGROUND
OF THE WAY TO MEET AS CHRISTIANS

According to Acts chapters two and five, the way to meet as Christians developed from the way the Jews met in the Old Testament. In Deuteronomy 12, God told the people of Israel through Moses that when they entered the land of Canaan, they should not meet and worship in any place that pleased them. Rather, they should wait until God chose and designated a place in the good land for them (vv. 5, 13-14). Subsequently, God chose Mount Zion in Jerusalem and designated that place as the unique place where the people of Israel were to meet together: "Three times a year all your males shall appear before Jehovah your God in the place which He will choose" (16:16). And the people of Israel did so; three times a year they all gathered in Jerusalem. There is no hint in the Old Testament that there were any small meetings besides these big meetings.

Later, the people of Israel in their degradation were taken captive and carried away to foreign lands, far from the holy temple. History tells us that in those Gentile lands the Jews built synagogues for themselves in which they assembled to read the Pentateuch and expound the Old Testament. That was the origin of the practice of Scripture reading on the Sabbath in the synagogues. This custom was brought from the land of captivity to the land of their ancestors to which they returned. When they first returned, the temple had not yet been rebuilt, so on the Sabbath they continued to go to the synagogues for Scripture reading and exposition of the books of Moses. According to Jewish history and New Testament records, the Jews did not forsake the practice of reading the Scriptures in the synagogues on the Sabbath, a practice which they initiated while they were in captivity in the Gentile lands, even after the rebuilding of the temple had been completed.

After the birth of the Lord Jesus and while John the Baptist was going forth to preach the word, these synagogues still existed. At that time there were numerous synagogues apart from the temple. Furthermore, they could be found not only in Jerusalem but also in Capernaum, in Galilee, and in many other places. Therefore, while the Lord Jesus was carrying out His ministry, He went to the synagogues, not to keep the Sabbath nor to worship God but merely to take the opportunity to preach to the Jews while they were gathered there (Luke 4:15).

Acts 2:1 says, "And as the day of Pentecost was being fulfilled." The Feast of Pentecost was one of the three great feasts of the Jews. On the day of Pentecost all the Jews in every place in the land gathered in Jerusalem; even the Jews who were in dispersion in the Gentile lands had to return to Jerusalem. Therefore, Acts 2:5 says that the Jews came back from their dispersion from every nation under heaven; some of them could not even speak the Jewish language but could only speak their own dialects. Therefore, there was the need of speaking in tongues. On the day of Pentecost while the people were all together in the same place, the Holy Spirit descended and Peter preached the gospel to the crowd. As a result, three thousand were saved. Once they were saved, they came out of the Jewish religion. This was what the Lord Jesus referred to in John 10, that He would lead His sheep out of the fold that they might become one flock under one Shepherd (v. 16), that is, to form them into one church. Once a person was baptized and left the Jewish religion, he became part of the church. As soon as the church began, the meetings from house to house were brought forth.

This shows us that the big meetings in the temple were not the church meetings; rather, the church meetings were the meetings from house to house. Today if we rented a large conference facility and gathered thousands of people so that we could preach the gospel to them, that would not be considered a church meeting. That would only be a big gathering in the temple for gaining people through the preaching of the gospel. If out of ten thousand who came, five hundred were saved and baptized, these five hundred then would be given to the church. Following this, they should meet from house to house as the church. This is the origin and background of the way to meet as Christians.

ADVANTAGES OF SMALL GROUP MEETINGS

Due to the degradation of the church, the way of meeting from house to house was completely lost, and thus, the church had no way to propagate and increase. Meeting from house to house has many advantages. On the day of Pentecost the newly saved and baptized ones all became constituents of the church and were then distributed to meet in different homes. Among the saints at that time, about one hundred and twenty, such as Peter and Mary, were somewhat experienced. These one hundred and twenty people could have taken care of only a hundred and twenty homes at the most; there was no one to take care of and lead the remaining homes. Therefore, this afforded the Holy Spirit a great opportunity to do a particular work so that the newly saved ones would all be led by the Holy Spirit.

Hence, the first advantage of the small group meeting is that it gives the Holy Spirit the opportunity to work. If in a meeting everything is prearranged, then there is no opportunity for the Holy Spirit to do any work. In the traditional Christian worship service, everything is prearranged; the program sheet clearly prints what time the service begins, who reads the Scriptures, which pastor leads the prayer, who preaches the sermon, who sings the solo, and so forth. Since everything is prearranged, the Holy Spirit has no opportunity to work at all. We must realize that in the small group meeting the Holy Spirit has the opportunity to work; therefore, we need to allow the Holy Spirit to work freely.

The second advantage of the group meeting is that in it the saints are able to know each other. Because the number is small, they are able to know each other and care for each other. Third, the group meeting creates plenty of opportunities for every saved person to develop the grace he has obtained and to manifest the gift he has received in the Holy Spirit. Fourth, the group meeting provides the greatest opportunity for everyone to function. We need to do this at the very beginning of the church life; otherwise, once a habit is formed, it will be hard to change in the future.

Besides all these, the group meeting also has the advantage of making it easy to lead people to salvation. Formerly, when a person wanted to be baptized, he had to pass through an interview, and the elders had to designate someone to baptize him and assign another one to be in charge of the baptism. Now with the small groups, every group can preach the gospel, the gospel can be widely preached, and the number of saved ones can increase rapidly. With so many to baptize, it would not work, nor would it be sufficient, to depend on arrangements. Therefore, wherever there is water for baptism, we can baptize people. We absolutely believe that if the churches would divide into small groups in a good way, we could bring in thousands of saved ones.

THE CHRISTIAN WAY OF MEETING
NEEDING TO BE TWO-SIDED

According to the Scriptures, the Christian way of meeting has to be two-sided. On one side are the big meetings, and on the other side are the small group meetings. These two sides are just like the two wings of an eagle, which are the same size and are balanced. Here let us consider not only church meetings but also all kinds of Christian meetings. Some Christian meetings seem to be church meetings, but they do not possess the definite nature of the church meetings. On the day of Pentecost, Peter's preaching to the people cannot be considered a church meeting. It did not have the nature of the church because at that moment the church had not been produced. After Peter finished preaching the gospel, three thousand people believed and were baptized. Once these three thousand were baptized, they were baptized into the church, and thus the church was produced. Then they began to meet from house to house; those meetings were church meetings. Therefore, the big meetings usually do not bear the nature of the church.

Big meetings are for bringing in people. This was what the Lord Jesus and the apostles did; they gained many people by making use of any available time and place. Frequently this meant preaching the gospel in the synagogues on the Sabbath. The apostle Paul also did this often in Acts. Today our convenient time is the Lord's Day. The whole world is under the influence of Christianity, and every Sunday—the day that Christians call the Lord's Day—ninety percent of the shops, factories, schools, and offices are closed for rest. This has become the common practice over almost the whole world, including even the Communist countries. Therefore, the Lord's Day is a day when people have leisure time. We should use this day to release the truth, just like the Lord Jesus did in preaching on the Sabbath in the synagogues.

Although we hope to change the system of our meetings by paying more attention to the group meetings, we should not forsake this one day—the Lord's Day. We should use the Lord's Day to have big meetings for the release of the truth or for gospel preaching to gain people. Hence, we may call the meeting on the Lord's Day the truth meeting. The Lord's Day can be for releasing the truth. Releasing the truth includes preaching the gospel, leading people to salvation, edifying the saints, and helping them to grow in life. These are all related to the release of the truth.

A FEW PROPOSALS
CONCERNING THE MEETING ON THE LORD'S DAY

For this kind of practice we have a few proposals. First, we should have a meeting to take care of those who want to listen to messages. Throughout the world people have the custom of going to church and listening to sermons. No matter how much we stand against the traditions and old habits of Christianity, there will still be some people who want to go to a meeting hall on the Lord's Day to worship God and listen to sermons. We cannot condemn people who have this habit, because the Lord Himself went to preach in the synagogues on the Sabbath. He went not to keep the Sabbath, nor to read the Scriptures; He went into the synagogues to take the opportunity to release the truth. Therefore, we should keep this principle. Regardless of what we do, on the Lord's Day we should have a meeting in the meeting hall for people to worship God and listen to a sermon. We need to take care of this category of people. The messages should cover topics of general interest and should be neither too shallow nor too deep. Every church should have this kind of provision.

Second, we should teach the truth on the Lord's Day, and we should separate into different levels. More than thirty years ago in Taiwan we brought in many young people within one or two years, and almost all of them were college graduates. Now their children have graduated from college, and some have even obtained doctorate degrees. Yet, spiritually, the parents have not yet graduated from elementary school. Although they have been listening to messages at the meeting hall every Lord's Day for more than thirty years, they have not yet graduated from spiritual elementary school; this is a great problem. The reason for this is that although they have been listening to "famous preachers" for thirty years, they have not attended classes on the fundamental lessons. This is our situation, and it is the same everywhere.

In recent years we have surely advanced in the truth. We not only know spiritual addition, subtraction, multiplication, and division, we have even learned algebra and calculus. We can see that we are of a learned family, especially in the prayers of the saints. However, we have to go one step further and ask ourselves if we could teach others the truth, such as the meaning of justification by faith. Perhaps all we can say is that to be justified by faith is to be saved without paying a price, that it is to obtain salvation freely and not by works, and that as long as we believe in the Lord Jesus, we are justified by faith. This kind of speaking will not easily convince people.

If we would study addition and subtraction in today's elementary schools, we would discover that now there are special methods of teaching and learning. Those of us in the older generation may know how to add and subtract, but if we were to learn them in today's schools, they might be different from what we learned before. Consider justification by faith for example. Perhaps we can only say that to be justified by faith is to receive salvation without paying a price, not having to rely on our works but relying only on our faith, and that as long as we call "O Lord Jesus," we will be saved and justified. It is hard to convince others with this kind of speaking. We must be able to explain in a logical and clear way the matter of justification by faith according to its proper meaning and line of thought in the Bible. Then people will be convinced and believe.

The young people in particular must learn the truth. First Timothy 2:4 says, "[God] desires all men to be saved and to come to the full knowledge of the truth." The Greek word rendered *full knowledge* means "a thorough and complete understanding"; it is not just to understand a little but to understand thoroughly. Suppose you are an eighteen-year-old sister. After being saved, you want very much to preach the gospel to your relatives, including your grandfather and grandmother who are against Christianity. When you go home, no matter how much they oppose, they cannot completely refuse to listen since you are their granddaughter. Therefore, you have to speak to them, telling them how the Lord Jesus accomplished redemption for us so that we could obtain forgiveness through Him and be justified before God. When you speak to them in such a logical way, outwardly your grandparents may still oppose you, but within they will feel that you are brilliant and will wonder where you learned such logical things. If necessary, you could also open the Bible and quote some verses to support your explanation. If you take this way, people cannot help but be convinced and believe.

After a period of time, when you go home and see your grandparents again, you can speak to them about the God of glory, the unique God. After listening to your speaking, they may feel that you are really marvelous. Your grandmother, who previously opposed you, may "run out of steam" and may not oppose you that much any more. Your grandfather may feel that what you are speaking about really makes sense. Then after another two weeks you can go home and speak again. In this way your previously unbelieving grandparents will eventually believe in the Lord.

We must believe that the truth can subdue people and that the truth will eventually prevail. The problem is that we, the saved ones, only go to church every week and listen to "famous preachers" but do not properly attend classes. Suppose there were a school today that had no classes, no teachers, and no textbooks. For six years the principal only arranged for famous speakers to give lectures every day. We can imagine that the students who graduated from this school would have surely heard a lot, but probably they would have no real abilities. Therefore, we have to change our system; instead of listening to "famous speakers," we must properly attend classes and seriously learn the truth.

COMPILING *TRUTH LESSONS* FOR THE SAINTS TO BE EDUCATED IN THE TRUTH TOGETHER

To help us learn the truth, we have specifically assigned three co-workers to form an editorial group to compile a book called *Truth Lessons*. We hope to have at least four levels: Level One, Level Two, Level Three, and Level Four, each level being progressively deeper than the previous one. Each level will have forty-eight lessons, sufficient material for a whole year. Four lessons will be covered every month, and the lessons for every three months will be combined into one volume. Thus, each volume will contain twelve lessons. Each level will consist of four volumes—one volume for spring, summer, fall, and winter respectively. Thus, there will be a total of forty-eight lessons in one year.

The contents of Level One, Volume 1, will cover various topics beginning with the Bible. Lesson 1 will be on the Bible; lesson 2, the Triune God; lesson 3, God's creation; lesson 4, Satan's origin and rebellion; lesson 5, man's fall; and lesson 6, God's promise of redemption. Then we will go on to cover a key view of the entire Old Testament. After the key view of the Old Testament, there will be a lesson on the difference between the New Testament and the Old Testament, and then we will go on to the key view of the New Testament. It will take half a year to finish the first two volumes. Then in the second half of the year, there will still be twenty-four more lessons. They will cover God's salvation, beginning with God's foreknowledge, selection, and predestination; continuing through man's being called, saved, and baptized into and joined to the Triune God; and concluding with man's being forgiven, justified, and sanctified, and how to be saved and baptized. All these topics will be included in these volumes. This will be the content of the forty-eight lessons in the first year.

We should teach the brothers and sisters one lesson after another, and there should be different levels of classes. The first level should be one class, the second level, another class, the third level, another class, and the fourth level, another class. The church should make arrangements in this matter without putting pressure on anyone. For instance, perhaps some saints have been meeting for eighteen years, yet they want to start from the beginning, from elementary school. If so, they may go to level one. If others want to go a little deeper, then they may go to level three or level four. We should prepare different classrooms so that all the saints can receive the education of the truth according to their own need.

In this way all the saints will be able to function. Today the nations are all endeavoring to create employment opportunities. By changing our system we will enable many to become "employed." Previously in Taipei, there were only twenty-one preachers in twenty-one halls; however, after changing the system, even fifty people will not be enough. This is because for one meeting hall we might need five or six people to teach the lessons; therefore, for twenty-one meeting halls we would need more than one hundred people to be "employed." The problem, however, is that some of the saints have reacted, saying that they do not know how to speak and to teach. Concerning this matter, we have considered holding a training and a presentation of teaching methods for the teachers of the truth lessons. We know that even apprentices in the barbershop need several tries before they can learn successfully. Everything is difficult at the beginning, but if we learn by doing, we will quickly learn to do it well.

There is a Chinese maxim which says that "the young hold potential for greatness." I hope that all the young people will rise up and put forth their effort. If they would do this, the situation would be so tremendous that people may not be able to withstand it. Ever since my grandchildren started school, whenever they come home, they like to teach me; they talk about history and science, and my head spins. Nonetheless, I am inwardly happy because it is a good sign. If the church has one thousand saints and all of them learn the truth and preach the truth, then the truth will surely prevail.

MINISTERING THE WORD OF GOD
IN VARIOUS MEETINGS

In the truth meeting on the Lord's Day, sometimes there may be unbelievers in attendance. In such a situation we should arrange a gospel meeting at that moment to meet their need. This would require certain ones to be ready; once they see that ten or twenty persons have come to listen to the gospel, they should invite them into a room prepared beforehand. We need to have some brothers preaching the gospel and others serving and helping people there. This is the church—everyone functions and everyone has the opportunity to be employed.

Besides this, after every baptism we should immediately arrange a new believers' edification meeting for the newly baptized ones. A newly baptized believer does not know a great deal of truth. In this kind of meeting, which is best to hold on the Lord's Day, we should teach them the truths related to new believers, such as what to do after being baptized, knowing the church, reading the Bible, and prayer. We need to teach them these things topic by topic. The church ought to release a great deal of truths on the Lord's Day so that the saints can learn the truths on their days off and in their spare time.

Furthermore, every Lord's Day, preferably in the evening, we should come together to remember the Lord. In addition, in the middle of the week we should have a prayer meeting, and on the weekends, either on Friday or Saturday, we should have a small group meeting. In this way every week we would have three meetings: the Lord's table, the prayer meeting, and the small group meeting. On the Lord's Day after the Lord's table, we should leave about half an hour for a brother who has prepared beforehand to lead all the saints in reading a message together which covers a specific topic. We do not need to spend too much time to read; the best way is to read one message thoroughly in twenty or thirty minutes. All this has to be carefully prepared ahead of time. We could let everybody know a week ahead so that they could prepare the pertinent books to be read together in the meeting. If the message is short, instead of asking the saints to bring the book, we can make copies for them to read together and to fellowship over together. In this way, for fifty-two weeks a year, on fifty-two Lord's Days, we could have fifty-two life-supplying messages.

The same principle should apply to the prayer meeting on Tuesday evening. We should leave about half an hour to read some materials prepared beforehand on the truth, preferably those materials that are related to spiritual service. In the latter part of the Lord's table we should have life-supplying messages, and in the second half of the prayer meeting we should cover some spiritual principles concerning service. In this way every week the saints will gain one life-supplying message and also learn some spiritual principles for service. In the long run everyone can go deeper and be perfected.

On Friday or Saturday we should have the small group meeting. Concerning the materials for the group meeting, the best thing to do may be to select one book from the life-study of the twenty-seven books of the New Testament that would suit the need of the church in your locality, and then arrange for someone to take charge. Do not read word by word, sentence by sentence; rather, the one who is in charge should prepare ahead of time to find out the important points, and then when he comes to the group meeting, he should use these crucial points for the saints to pray-read, fellowship, and share. I believe that such a definite help will be very enriching.

If the saints are faithful, week after week, fifty-two weeks a year, they can obtain a thorough knowledge of the truth, gain the supply of life, and receive guidance concerning service. Besides these, in the small group meetings they can have the mutual care, they can all exercise their function, and they can preach the gospel and lead people to salvation. In this way we will be able to take care of all the aspects.

Although we may use materials published by the Taiwan Gospel Book Room, this does not mean that we should let go of the Bible. The aim of all the publications of the Taiwan Gospel Book Room, particularly the *Life-study of the New Testament* and the Recovery Version of the New Testament, is to bring people to the Lord and to the Word as soon as they open a volume. We hope that through reading these books we could be brought into the Lord and into His Word. I believe that all these meetings will not waste our time.

The church should also have a big gospel meeting every two months. If the meeting hall does not have sufficient seating capacity, we should rent a bigger meeting facility. In these special gospel meetings, it would be best to ask one or two saints to give their testimonies and to ask another one to receive the burden to release a message. For a series of gospel messages, the book *Gospel Outlines* may be quite useful. This book contains a total of two hundred and sixty-four choice gospel subjects selected from every book of the Old and New Testaments, from Genesis through Revelation. When you use this book, there is no need to always use the whole portion of a subject; you may use one half of the material of one subject and another half of the material of another subject, thus combining two subjects into one message. That book can surely supply a great deal of gospel material, and it can also provide us with many points and lines on the gospel.

I hope that from now on in every meeting the saints would not just give a message according to what pleases them. We all must enter into the depths of the truth; otherwise, we will not be able to minister to the saints in the meeting. We may illustrate in this way. When a teacher is teaching, he cannot just talk as he does ordinarily, speaking words "off the top of his head." That would be irresponsible. Before he teaches, he must properly prepare the lesson. Furthermore, in his preparation, he must prepare according to the textbook; he cannot just gather any material he likes outside of the textbook. Today the lines have all been laid out. Whether for gospel lessons, for prayer, or for the Lord's table, the guidelines have been pointed out to you. You have to enter into the depths; then eventually the content of your speaking will be the riches of the truth. In this way, after a period of time all the local churches will be rich in truth and vigorous in life.

Chapter Six

PROBLEMS TO AVOID IN SPEAKING FOR GOD

We know that the purpose of all Christian meetings is to speak Christ. However, first we must pay attention to the fact that in order to speak Christ we must have the experience of Christ. We will not know where to start speaking unless we have the experience of Christ. Second, regardless of what we speak about, we need to utter and express it with words; therefore, we need to have the knowledge of the truth. Christ is the mystery of God. To God, He is the mystery of God; to us, He is wisdom and power from God. These items—mystery, wisdom, and power—are not shallow matters. Hence, to speak these things we must know the truth, that is, we must have the words to make known the truth. Without experience and truth, even if we wanted to speak, we would have no way to start. Without the experience of Christ and the knowledge of the truth, we have nothing to speak about or enunciate.

NEEDING TO KNOW THE TRUTH SYSTEMATICALLY

Because truth is not only a matter of the truth itself but also a matter of life, it has two aspects. Truth is not only for our utterance; it is also for the opening of our mind. To others, truth is an expression of something passing through us, but to us, truth is an opening. If there were no truth, how could we know Christ? If there were no truth, how could our understanding be opened, therefore making it possible for us to experience Christ? Without the truth, how could we understand Christ as the mystery of God? Without the truth, how could we experience Christ as wisdom and power from God to us? Without the truth, we would have no way to know and experience Christ practically.

We all know that we are very rich in truth; however, the degree or level of our knowledge of the truth is not very high. In most people's eyes we have a rich spiritual heritage because we have the publications, the conferences, and the trainings, all of which impart a great deal of knowledge to us. However, we have not helped the saints to learn the truth in a systematic way. We are always asking "famous speakers" to give "lectures" to the saints, but we have never set up a course of instruction and invited some teachers to teach the saints truth lessons in a systematic way.

Consider today's educational system as an example. When a child reaches the age of four or five, he goes to kindergarten to learn some basic knowledge so that he may formally go to the regular school. When he is six years old, he begins to learn the lessons in the first grade, then second grade, third grade, fourth grade, fifth grade, and sixth grade, until he graduates from elementary school. Then he can take courses in junior high school. If there were no such system of going to classes but only lectures given by famous guest speakers, then after listening for eight, nine, or even ten years, the children would not even be able to pass the entrance exam to middle school because they would not have the specific, orderly, and thorough knowledge of the contents of what they heard.

This matter has delayed us in many respects and has also deeply affected our spreading, increase, and multiplication. From the time we started the work here in Taiwan in 1949 to the present time, we have baptized more than 100,000 people, yet the number of those who remain and are meeting regularly is less than 10,000 in all of Taiwan. The church in Taipei has about 5,000 saints who meet regularly, which is about one half of the number for all of the churches in Taiwan. Among nearly one hundred churches in Taiwan, the number of those who regularly meet and those who alternately meet with us is less than 15,000. From these statistics we see that at least seventy or eighty thousand of those who were baptized are wandering outside instead of remaining in the church life. This is because we have not had the proper education in the truth; as a result, we have not been able to take care of the newly saved ones nor retain them in a proper way.

CHRISTIANS SPEAKING FOR GOD
TO VARIOUS KINDS OF PEOPLE

Therefore, after much consideration, we feel that we have no alternative but to change the system. The way to carry out this change must be in two aspects. On the one hand, we need to speak for God among ourselves in the meetings of the church, and on the other hand, we need to speak for God to the outsiders outside of the church meetings. In the church meetings there are relatively fewer people to whom we can speak for God, but outside the meetings there are many to whom we can speak. First, we can speak to those who have been baptized but have not yet been brought into the church life. After less than one year since we changed the system, we already have more than 3,000 newly baptized ones in Taipei alone. However, among these 3,000 only about 310 have been brought into the church life. There are over 2,000 who are still outside of the church life; thus, there is the need for us to go and speak to them.

Second, we have to speak to the unsaved ones. Acts 16:31 says, "Believe on the Lord Jesus, and you shall be saved, you and your household." Today is your whole family saved? I believe that many family members among you are not yet saved, so you have to go to your relatives and friends and speak the Lord's word to them. First go to your close relatives, then your distant relatives, and then your friends. The definition of what a *friend* is, is very broad. It includes your neighbors, your colleagues, and your schoolmates. All your acquaintances are counted as friends. Even the people on the street could become your friends; after you talk to them for three or five minutes, they become your friends. Therefore, the term *friend* has a very broad definition.

In Acts 1:8, the Lord Jesus says, "But you shall receive power when the Holy Spirit comes upon you, and you shall be My witnesses both in Jerusalem and in all Judea and Samaria and unto the uttermost part of the earth." We may interpret this verse in this way: *Jerusalem* refers to our close relatives; *all Judea,* our distant relatives; *Samaria,* our neighbors; and *the uttermost part of the earth,* all of our friends. We all have some close relatives, such as our parents and our siblings; these are our Jerusalem. Our distant relatives, such as our cousins, aunts, and uncles, are our Judea. The neighbors and colleagues around us are our Samaria. Besides all these, the friends we see everywhere are our uttermost part of the earth. Therefore, there is no end to preaching the gospel to the unsaved ones.

Third, we have to speak to Christians in general. They are our brothers and sisters, except that they are not meeting with us. In the past we referred to them as Christians in the denominations. From now on I hope that we will avoid using this kind of expression. When we say that they are those who belong to the denominations, it sounds like they are of one sect and we are of another. This is not good; this is not proper. They would not like us to refer to them as such. Since we are all brothers and sisters in the Lord, we should not refer to them in such a discriminating way.

Therefore, we all must be careful not to use phrases such as "denominational Christians." They are our brothers and sisters because we all have the same Lord and were begotten of the same Father. When we come into contact with them, we have to speak the words of the truth to them. From the aforementioned points we can see that we have a great number of people to whom we can speak for God. Therefore, we need to pursue the truth seriously and be constituted with the words of the truth so that we may all go out and speak for God. This way will keep us from standing idle and afford us the opportunity to fully exercise our function.

SEPARATING INTO THE HOMES
TO BRING IN THE INCREASE

In our seeking before the Lord, we feel that the church in Taipei, the church in Singapore, the church in Manila, the church in Hong Kong, and even the church in Jakarta must all aim at having one thousand home meetings. Any locality with a population of more than three million must aim at dividing into one thousand small homes. Every small home should have eight to ten people, so one thousand homes will have eight to ten thousand people. We know that the more we divide into the homes, the more we multiply. Let us use a couple with ten children as an illustration. Suppose the parents keep all the children at home with them, so that the sons never marry and the daughters are never given in marriage. Eventually, the parents will get old, and the children will also become old. This situation is not normal.

If we release our sons and daughters, letting them marry, then there will be increase and propagation. Each additional marriage will afford one additional unit for reproduction. When three get married, there will be three units for reproduction; when seven get married, there will be seven units for reproduction. After a few years they will multiply to over twenty persons. Those who understand gardening know that in planting flowers, shrubs, or trees, it is hard for them to multiply if the farmer plants them close together, but if he separates them into groups, planting them in small groves, then they will multiply rapidly. Therefore, we must separate into homes; this will bring in the increase.

If we want everyone to function by preaching the truth for this kind of multiplication, then we must provide them an education on various levels. Only in this way can we raise up those who can preach the truth. Then in the Lord's Day morning meetings there will be no fear of having no one to give a message for the ministry of the word. If the elders take the lead to preach the Lord's word, then the saints will have a pattern to follow. When the saints see such a pattern, they will also go out to speak to others. Once this kind of atmosphere is started, the result will be that all the saints will be able to preach the Lord's word to those who are outside the church. Whether by proclaiming Christ, by expounding the Holy Scriptures, or by releasing the truth, after three to five years, their preaching will be able to cover all the districts in their locality. This is the Lord's way.

Satan, who is very cunning, prevents men from seeing the Lord's way. However, if we read Acts chapters two, four, and five, we can clearly see this principle of separating into homes. In the beginning the saints met from house to house (2:46). Then in chapter eight, due to the great persecution that came upon the church in Jerusalem, "all were scattered throughout the regions of Judea and Samaria, except the apostles" (v. 1).

Thus, the disciples were scattered among various towns and villages, and they all announced the word of God as the gospel (v. 4). After the disciples were dispersed, not only did they quickly spread throughout all of Judea, but they also reached Samaria. The record in chapter eight shows that in Samaria there were people who believed in the Lord. Afterward, Philip the evangelist also went there, and a church was raised up immediately.

This shows us that not long after they had been saved, the early believers in Jerusalem all became teachers, evangelists, and prophets. Moreover, when the churches were raised up, the believers also became apostles. If the local churches today would all practice this way, then the gospel would be preached rapidly throughout the entire earth. Whether in Taiwan, Southeast Asia, or the Western world, all would be gospelized rapidly. However, this all depends on whether or not we are willing to practice this and whether or not we do it right. If all of us are willing to practice this and we all do it right, then the result will be a success.

What we have fellowshipped should not be made into rules and regulations to be observed accordingly one by one. What we hope is that you would all bring this fellowship back with you for study and that you would pray much. If someone, after his study and prayer, can find a better way before the Lord, that would be wonderful. In principle, we need to help the saints by every means so that they all can understand the truth. God desires all men to be saved and to come to the full knowledge of the truth. Not only so, we also need to help the saints so that they all could go forth and be prophets speaking for the Lord.

FACING VARIOUS PROBLEMS
IN OUR SPEAKING FOR GOD

We would like to fellowship concerning some of the things we should absolutely avoid when we speak for God. Those who know a little about farming know that when a farmer farms his field, there are certain things he must avoid so that the growth of the crop will not be hampered. First he must protect his crop against floods. Then he must protect against insects, that is, he must prevent the insects from eating up the tender sprouts in the field. In farming, the hardest problem is how to deal with the various kinds of insects. Once you plant some trees, there will be insects; one kind of tree will have this kind of insect, while another kind of tree will have another kind of insect. While some of the insects are easy to deal with, others are very hard to deal with and cannot be killed regardless of how hard you try. Eventually you may have to burn the tree down, but that is really the worst strategy. Therefore, we have to avoid the harm caused by insects.

In Song of Songs the Lord says, "Catch the foxes for us, / The little foxes, / That ruin the vineyards / While our vineyards are in blossom" (2:15). Here we see that the little foxes come to damage especially when the vineyards are in blossom. We also may discover harmful pests called snails. They particularly eat the flower buds; they do not eat the leaves or the stem, but they specifically eat the best and most tender parts. Furthermore, after eating the buds, they hide themselves so that you are unable to find them.

The little foxes do not come when the vine is not in blossom; it is when the vine is in blossom that they come. Now at this time we are going forward, and the vineyards will soon be in blossom. Once they blossom, we have to be on guard against the coming of the little foxes. This is what we have to avoid. The little foxes, snails, and other germs and pests will bring in damage. This requires our prevention. There is another animal called the gopher. Gophers are terrible because they burrow under the trees and create underground passageways. They live underground and secretly ruin the growth of many flowers, plants, trees, and crops. In Matthew 13, the Lord Jesus also used the birds and thorns as illustrations. He said that the sower went out to sow, but although the seeds were sown, they encountered all kinds of difficulties, such as being devoured by the birds of the air or being choked by the thorns, so that the seeds could not bear fruit (vv. 4, 7). Today we are experiencing these things, and we need to be warned.

Not Teaching Things Different
from God's Economy

The first warning is for the co-workers. An error which we who work for the Lord most easily make is that we like to give messages according to our preference. On the one hand, we prefer to give messages which fit our taste; on the other hand, we prefer not to speak others' messages. We would not "cook others' dishes," that is, we would not speak what others have already spoken. Almost every co-worker is like this. Therefore, in 1 Timothy 1 Paul told Timothy, "I exhorted you...to remain in Ephesus," and asked Timothy to especially pay attention to one thing: to "charge certain ones not to teach different things" (v. 3). In Paul's time, the "different things" referred first to the law, which was of and according to the Old Testament. Second, they referred to the genealogies, especially the research of the Old Testament genealogies. All these are according to the Old Testament, but they are things which are different from the New Testament economy.

Then in verse 4 Paul continued to say, "Which produce questionings rather than God's economy, which is in faith." In other words, the "different things" taught by those people were not according to God's economy. God's economy is firstly Christ as the mystery of God, and secondly the church as the mystery of Christ. From the fourteen Epistles written by Paul we can see that the focus of the messages he preached was Christ and the church. Today the things being taught in Christianity may be scriptural, yet there are too many different teachings. One example is the practice of foot-washing. Foot-washing is surely according to the Bible. In America there are Christians who insist that the believers must wash each other's feet before they break the bread; however, there are some who do not practice this, thus giving rise to debates. Some Christians often debate concerning scriptural practices such as head covering, baptism, and the Lord's table and are therefore divided from each other.

In 1933, Brother Watchman Nee began publishing a little magazine called *Collection of Newsletters,* mainly to publish the fellowship among the churches raised up by the Lord in various places in China. Due to the lack of correspondence, the churches were not receiving news of each other, so Brother Nee published this magazine to allow the churches to receive this news. He was the editor, and when he was busy on a trip, he would ask Sister Ruth Lee to be the acting editor. In 1934, the second year of its publication, Sister Lee also took a trip, so he asked me to be the acting editor. That year there was a great deal of fellowship; letters from different localities were continually flooding in. All these letters, however, repeatedly referred to things such as leaving the denominations, baptism, head covering, and the breaking of bread. As the acting editor, I selected eight or ten good ones and published them. After reading them, Brother Nee, who was in Foochow at that time, immediately wrote me a letter, saying, "Brother Witness, do not publish in the *Collection of Newsletters* things concerning leaving the denominations, baptism, head covering, and the breaking of bread."

After that, Brother Nee also asked me to co-sign a statement with him saying that "if any co-worker goes out to specifically speak about things such as head covering, bread breaking, and baptism, then he is no longer our co-worker." Concerning this matter, some asked, "Was it not Brother Nee who taught us head covering?" For sure Brother Nee taught this, and not only he taught this but the apostle Paul also did. In 1 Corinthians 11 Paul gave us this teaching, but he linked this teaching to Christ. He said, "Christ is the head of every man, and the man is the head of the woman, and God is the head of Christ" (v. 3). Hence, the sisters should have their head covered. Paul's teaching of head covering was linked to Christ. Today, however, people teach head covering as something detached from Christ; this is to teach differently.

Among Christians, there are many debates concerning baptism. There are endless arguments even on what kind of water to use. Should we use water from the faucet, water from the river, or water from the sea? Should it be cold water or warm water? Should it be fresh water or salt water? Some pastors even say that the scriptural way is to go and be baptized in the river of Jordan as the Lord Jesus was. Even more absurd is that some in the United States are discussing how

many times a person should be immersed—once or three
times? Those who advocate the practice of being immersed
three times base their argument on the Lord's word in the
Gospel of Matthew that we have to baptize people into the
name of the Father, the Son, and the Holy Spirit (28:19).
Therefore, they say that we need to immerse people once in
the name of the Father, once in the name of the Son, and once
in the name of the Holy Spirit and that only then is the baptism complete. Others ask about the way to baptize people.
Should we baptize them leaning backward, leaning forward, or
leaning sideways? These things produce many questionings
among Christians, causing people to become confused. This
shows us that although there are many teachings among
Christians and although these teachings are all from the
Scriptures, they are different teachings and are even strange.

The central teaching in the New Testament is the economy of God, which is concerning Christ as the mystery of
God and the church as the mystery of Christ; Christ and
the church are the great mystery. This is the message we
preach. By the Lord's mercy, we have not preached anything
other than Christ and the church in our speaking and in our
publications. In other words, we only preach that Christ as
the mystery of God expresses God and that the church as the
mystery of Christ expresses Christ. In speaking the economy
of God we follow the example of Paul. However, at the time
of Paul there were some who did not preach this economy;
therefore, Paul charged Timothy to pay attention to this
matter. In the same way, some of our so-called co-workers also
do not like to speak about God's economy; they like to speak
only their own messages.

When people preach according to their own preferences,
this causes problems. For example, Apollos was one who especially knew the Scriptures and was especially able to expound
the Scriptures. However, Apollos had a problem in his preaching and eventually was not in the same stream as Paul was
(Acts 18:24-25; 19:1-7; cf. 1 Cor. 16:12). We all must see this
matter clearly. Therefore, the co-workers must avoid this kind
of problem; what we speak must be in the same one burden. I
co-labored with Brother Nee for eighteen years. In all those

years I absolutely did not speak my own messages. Whatever message Brother Nee spoke, I spoke the same. Not only did I not make any changes, but I even clearly told people that this was a message given by Brother Nee in such and such a place and on such and such a day. This is not to say that I did not have any messages of my own and therefore had to speak Brother Nee's messages. I had quite a number of messages that I could have spoken, but I purposely did not do it. I spoke only what Brother Nee spoke, because I saw clearly that that was the Lord's recovery at the time.

At present, the same kind of problem exists in all the localities—we are not in perfect harmony. Although we do not harbor any evil intentions against each other, everyone is speaking according to his own preference. As a result, in the church it appears that there are two trumpets, which produces an uncertain sound. An army can have only one trumpet; then the whole army will have a unified command. If there are two trumpet sounds, even if one of them is very weak, it will cause a problem.

The Greek word for *truth* is *aletheia,* a word which is quite difficult to explain. It is used more than one hundred times in the New Testament. There is a very good Greek dictionary—*Theological Dictionary of the New Testament*—which explains every word in the New Testament. It was written in German by a German brother whose last name was Kittel. The entire New Testament uses more than 7,600 Greek words, and Kittel's research puts them into ten big volumes, clearly indicating the usage of every Greek word. He explains the changes in their meanings from their most ancient uses to their classical usages. He also gives clear explanations of how the words were used when the Greek language pervaded the Mediterranean region. Not only so, in these volumes he also discusses the meanings of each word as used in the New Testament writings, as well as their meanings in ordinary usage outside of the biblical writings. From this book we see that Greek words have different usages according to five periods of time. Kittel points out all these usages for us. Because of this book we can get to the depths and carefully study every book of the New Testament.

Take the word *truth* for example. In the New Testament usage this word has eight meanings, all of which are clearly written in note 6 of 1 John 1:6 of the Recovery Version of the New Testament. We only need to enter into this footnote diligently to obtain its riches. When we study the truth, what we need to do is read the Recovery Version and life-study messages carefully. This is because what was written in them did not come out of our imagination. What we wrote is absolutely based on the meaning of the Greek text and is according to the truth.

From the time Brother Watchman Nee laid the foundation of the truth for us until now, the Lord's recovery has been among us for over sixty years. These sixty years may be divided into two periods. The first period, from 1922 to 1952, covers the first thirty years, which was the period of Brother Nee's ministry. In 1922 Brother Nee started the first meeting of the Lord's recovery in Foochow, and in 1952 he was put into prison. This period of exactly thirty years was the period in which he released the truth. We came overseas in 1949, but we may say that in 1952 we formally started to release the truth, and until the present time it has been thirty years also. In the latter thirty years, the major part of the truth was released mainly through me.

The truths in these two periods are a perfect match and are all centered on Christ and the church. We have never deviated from this right track: Christ as the mystery of God and the church as the mystery of Christ being the economy of God and a great mystery. The thousands of messages we have spoken, regardless of how they were presented, were all concerning the economy of God. Therefore, I hope that all the saints among us would see this, and I especially hope that those who minister the word would no longer try to produce something "new."

Putting aside the riches of Brother Nee and the messages I have given, some among us have gone to the books of Christianity looking for some material to preach. This is really foolish. We have obtained the riches among us by standing on the shoulders of our predecessors, yet today some want to go and search for something under the feet of our predecessors.

What a pity this is! Since we are all human, of course we prefer to speak our own messages. However, we need to see what marvelous riches the Lord has given us and that what He wants us to preach is His economy only.

Whether we are older or younger, in the future we all may become teachers of the truth. May none of us try to speak "new things" by ourselves. What we speak must be concerning the economy of God—Christ and the church. Anything we speak apart from this economy is a different teaching and will result in much damage to the Lord's recovery. We must pay close attention to this matter.

Not Being the Head, Not Assuming Any Position, Not Monopolizing, and Not Controlling

The first warning is for the co-workers, and the second warning is for the elders. The common illness of the elders is that they love to be the head; they often feel that they are the owner and boss of their local church. Although no elder would say this, in reality this is exactly their feeling. This is a common sickness.

The record in Matthew 20 tells us that the Lord Jesus had two cousins, John and James, who were born of the sister of the mother of the Lord Jesus. One day their mother used this "apron-string" relationship to ask a favor from the Lord on her sons' behalf. She asked if the Lord could let her two sons, who were two cousins of the Lord Jesus, to sit with Him, one on the right and one on the left, when He received His kingdom (v. 21). Then the other ten disciples were indignant concerning the two brothers when they heard the request. Therefore, the Lord Jesus called these disciples together and said to them, "You know that the rulers of the Gentiles lord it over them....It shall not be so among you; but whoever wants to become great among you shall be your servant, and whoever wants to be first among you shall be your slave; just as the Son of Man did not come to be served, but to serve and to give His life as a ransom for many" (vv. 25-28). The Lord Himself served people to such an extent that He even gave His life as a ransom for many. Therefore, today we must not be those who exercise authority over others but those who serve others as servants.

Sisters, if your husband becomes an elder, I hope that you would not consider him to have become an official, as if it were something of an honor. You must realize that from that day onward, you have not become the first lady; rather, you have become the servant-lady. Brothers, you also have to be clear that even though you may have been used by the Lord to raise up a church, you cannot be the king there. Once you become the king, you will kill the church life completely. Once the elders become kings and heads, the church life will definitely be altogether finished. Therefore, I hope that the saints, particularly the brothers, would understand and remember well that no matter where you are, no matter how great the opportunity and how much grace the Lord has given to you, and no matter how much the Lord has used you, you should not be the head yourself.

The brothers not only should not be the head in the church, but even at home they should not assume the headship all the time. Otherwise, one day a storm will come, and there will be a revolution at home. Do not press the saints to such an extent that they secretly say, "What kind of heads are these elders? They are hatchet heads and ax heads!" This may be the situation within us. We have to avoid this. This is also one of the reasons why we cannot multiply and cannot increase.

The elders not only must not be the head and must not assume a position; furthermore, they must not monopolize and must not control. The matters in the church are corporate matters. Of course, if there are matters related to idol worship, then the elders cannot agree to it. Even if it means their martyrdom, this is proper. However, if the brothers have some suggestions regarding how to arrange the various services in the church, everyone can fellowship about them; it is not necessary to argue and be contentious. Although the opinions of some of the brothers might be strange, we still must bring them into the fellowship. In any case, do not monopolize everything and do not control.

The best way is for the elders to assign tasks to the saints and then to be responsible only to oversee them from the side.

The Bible says that the elders are overseers (1 Tim. 3:2). A certain elder may be very diligent—doing everything and even cleaning the restrooms himself. If you ask him why he does that, he may answer, "The brothers and sisters are so poor in their character that they cannot even clean the restrooms properly." The hidden meaning in his answer is that he is the only one who can clean the restrooms well, and therefore he has to do it himself. Hence, he is the one who polishes the windows, and he is also the one who makes phone calls for coordination. He does everything, just like a very able mother in the family. We all know that when a mother is too capable, the children usually are not capable. For instance, if a mother cooks very well, then the children can hardly cook a good meal because the mother does it all. Conversely, if a mother is not good in cooking, then she gives the children many opportunities to cook. As a result, the children become good cooks. This is a mysterious matter.

The more we hold on to everything and are unwilling to give others the opportunity to serve, the more we monopolize many things, and the result is that it is hard for others to function. A mother may have absolutely no thought or intention to hold on to everything. Everything she does is for her children; she does everything for them because they cannot do anything well. Nevertheless, she is holding on, that is, she is monopolizing. For a mother to be a good cook is a wonderful thing, but she also has to let the other members of her family have the opportunity to try and learn. Otherwise, they will never learn how to cook. The mother may be assured that even if their cooking is so poor that they turn the rice into paste, it is still all right. Today their cooking may be bad, but after tomorrow and the next day, and after practicing for a period of time, they will gradually learn the skills of cooking. Just as it is with the family, so it is with the church. In order for the church to spread and multiply, the elders absolutely must not grasp everything in their hand, because if they grasp everything, they are exercising control. Even though they may not say that they are controlling, they are still controlling. We must guard against and avoid these things.

In 1968 over one hundred and thirty saints from America

went to visit Taiwan. At that time, Hall 1 of the church in Taipei was rushing to finish constructing a five-story building on the north side; the cement was not yet completely dry when we arrived there. After we all entered the building, we discovered that all the restrooms were locked. When we asked about this, we found out that the keys had been taken by an elder to his office. It is incredible that an elder would control the church to such an extent. Eventually we found out that he wanted to reserve the newly built restrooms for the visitors from afar. Nonetheless, regardless of how valid the reason was, he should not have exercised control in that way. There should have been a permanent place to keep the keys, and the keys should have been numbered so that everyone would have known which key was for which restroom. If there had been such an arrangement, there would have been no confusion, and it also would have been very convenient. There is not just one person serving in the meeting hall; rather, there may be over a hundred serving ones there. Therefore, we need to let all the serving ones know what to do. In this way there will be no monopolizing or controlling. Rather, there will be a good administration.

The elders must take heed not to control. Even if the saints do not do things so well, it does not matter; eventually they will improve. Please remember not to argue. No matter what the saints propose, the elders must fellowship about it properly and not argue with them. The elders should never contend with others. All the elders have to learn this lesson. The Third Epistle of John refers to Diotrephes, who loved to be first, as an evil pattern (vv. 9-11). Therefore, in the church do not be those who love to be first. When a person loves to be first, that is evil. Those who reject others will eventually be rejected by others.

NOT FORMING PARTIES

The third warning is that we must not be divided into parties, and we must not ask people to follow us. Sometimes we may hear someone saying to another, "Brother, I am on your side." Such a word is neither spiritual nor sweet. We all have to learn not to draw others to our side and not to have any following. We also have to learn not to take sides with others. Forming parties is an act of the flesh. When the Corinthians were saying there that they were of Paul, of Apollos, of Cephas, or of Christ, Paul condemned them in his Epistle (1 Cor. 1:12). In the church there should be no factions. We are all of Christ, we are all brothers and sisters, and we are members one of another. You are my member, and I even the more am your member; we all are members of one another. Therefore, do not draw people to follow you, and do not follow anyone. This is to be absolutely condemned because it is detrimental to the church life; hence, we must surely guard against it.

Avoiding Being the Only One in the Lead

Fourth, whatever service or small group meeting we are in, we absolutely must not assume the headship. Although in every matter, it seems that someone needs to take the lead, we must avoid it by all means so that others may learn to take the lead. Even if the meeting becomes a little disorderly, it does not matter; at least it is better than we ourselves being the only one in the lead and monopolizing everything. Of course, it is not good to have the meeting in disorder. We hope that all of us will learn to trust in the Lord. Trusting in the Lord will save us from being disorderly. In the church there is only one Head—our Lord Jesus (11:3). Besides Him, we have no other head.

Avoiding Lengthy Speaking in the Meetings

Fifth, we must avoid speaking too many times or too long in the meetings. We must care for the sense of the meeting. For instance, if someone speaks eight times in a meeting, thus occupying most of the meeting time, this would be inappropriate. Furthermore, do not give a long discourse when speaking. Some may speak just once in the meeting, yet their speaking lasts thirty-five minutes; this is also not proper. We should also not pray long prayers in the prayer meeting. When a prayer is long, it kills the meeting. Once there was a brother in Shanghai who would always be present whenever there was a meeting, and whenever he was present, would always pray, and whenever he prayed, would always pray long. Whenever the saints saw him coming to the meeting, they were all worried and troubled, and whenever he opened his mouth, everybody simply could not stand it.

I once heard a story related to D. L. Moody. During Moody's time there was a person in the meetings who often prayed and would not stop. This afforded Moody an opportunity to learn a lesson, and he gained wisdom from it. He told the congregation, "While our brother keeps on praying without end, do not stop him, but let us just be dismissed." What Moody meant was, "Since he does not care about our feeling, we cannot do anything about him, so we just have to let him do what he is doing while we do what we should do." I hope that all of us would take heed to care for the sense of the meeting.

Avoiding Not Caring for the Atmosphere and Flow of the Meeting

Sixth, we must avoid not caring for the atmosphere and flow of the meeting. The Christian meeting has a flow, an atmosphere. What is the atmosphere of a meeting? For instance, the meeting today may be a wedding meeting, so the atmosphere of course is very joyous. Yet if someone comes in with sadness all over his face, then that would be rather inappropriate. Conversely, if we attend a funeral service, and everyone there is so sober, yet some of the attendants are very joyful, then that would also be improper. When we say that there is a flow of the meeting, we mean that there is a center of fellowship in the meeting. One of the saints may be quiet in the meeting most of the time, but once he decides to open his mouth, he always speaks something contrary to the atmosphere of the meeting. When everyone is fellowshipping in joy, he rebukes; when everyone is sharing about something sad, he laughs. This is to not care for the atmosphere and to not follow the flow of the meeting.

We have said already that the Christian meeting may be likened to a basketball game. Each team has five players, so there are ten people playing in the game, but they have only one ball and can use only that ball. This is the rule. However, one of the players may simply ignore this rule, so while the game is going on, he is playing with another ball by himself on the side and is even enjoying it. The same situation is frequently seen in the meeting. A certain brother may stand up and speak something of his own and may go on speaking until it is impossible for the meeting to proceed, yet he continues to enjoy his own speaking, caring neither for the atmosphere nor the flow of the meeting. We must not do this. We all love the Lord, the church, and the meetings. Yet when we come to the meeting we must care for the atmosphere and the flow of the meeting. We must not put on a one-man show, not caring for others' feelings; this will easily bring in death.

If while we are speaking in the meeting, we become aware that no one is saying amen, then we must stop our speaking as soon as possible. We have to care for the atmosphere of the meeting, and we also must care for others' feelings and not waste others' time. Suppose there are five hundred brothers and sisters meeting together. If you speak for ten minutes, and all five hundred speak for ten minutes each, then we would need five thousand minutes, which would be very time-consuming. We must take care of this point. We need to pay attention to this matter particularly in the small group meetings. He who ought to speak should speak quickly; he who ought not to speak should not speak that much. This is the key to whether or not the meeting will be living, fresh, and full of supply.

Avoiding Selecting Hymns and Bible Verses according to Our Own Taste

Seventh, we need to learn how to select hymns and Bible verses. When we select hymns and Bible verses, we must not do it according to our own taste. Whenever we come to a meeting, we should refrain from selecting our favorite hymn or Bible verse—the verse or hymn that we always select, regardless of whether the wind is blowing, the rain is coming down, or the sky is clear. We have to learn to sense the atmosphere of the meeting and to care for the flow of the meeting. We must not care only for our favorite hymn and favorite verse. For this we must be familiar with the hymns and study the

Bible well so that we can meet the need of the meeting. I hope that the young people would especially be familiar with the hymns and Bible passages so that you would be able to use them skillfully. Then when you come into the meeting, as soon as you detect the atmosphere of the meeting, you will be able to select a hymn or a portion of the Word which is fitting to that kind of atmosphere.

Caring for the Pleasant Feeling
Imparted in the Meeting

Eighth, we have to care for the pleasant feeling which the meeting imparts to people. A meeting must give people a kind of pleasant feeling, causing people to feel that this meeting is sweet. If in our meeting we act in a rough manner, we will lose the sense of sweetness. In the meeting we have to do everything in good order and in an orderly manner so that we may manifest the sweet and pleasant feeling of God's people meeting together with God in His presence. We need to maintain such a pleasant feeling in our meetings.

Caring for Others to Be Edified

In addition, we should avoid doing and speaking anything habitually without caring about whether or not others are edified.

Closely Following the Spirit

To conclude, in the matter of speaking for God, we must closely follow the Spirit. If we closely follow the Spirit, then the various problems mentioned above will be readily solved.

These points are merely introductory. I hope that we all would go before the Lord to see if there are any other matters that are improper or inappropriate. We must avoid all improper matters, not only in the meeting but even in the church life and in our homes. Our actions and behavior must be profitable to the church, must edify the saints, and must enable the way of the Lord to be gloriously released. If we do everything properly, then when we speak for the Lord, we will win people's respect, and the way of the Lord will spontaneously be glorified. If in our practice we would actively go forth to release the word of the Lord on the positive side, while avoiding all these problems on the negative side, then the Lord will surely have a way on the earth.

CHAPTER SEVEN

THE WAY TO SPEAK FOR THE LORD OUTSIDE OF THE CHURCH MEETINGS

THE BUDGET AND OUTLOOK FOR THE ADVANCE OF THE CHURCH

For the church to advance there is the need to increase and spread. Without the increase and the spread, the church has no way to advance. The way for the church to increase includes two steps: first, frequently preaching the gospel so that people can be saved and brought to the Lord; second, bringing the saved ones solidly into the church life. This is the increase, and only when there is the increase can there be the spreading outward. In these years, although the churches have been increasing and spreading, the increase and the spread have been too slow.

For example, twenty years ago the total number of saints in the churches in Southeast Asia was at least 2,000. There were at least 500 to 800 saints in Indonesia twenty years ago. Among the churches there, Surabaya was the biggest one and had around 200 saints in 1965. The second largest was Jakarta, the third was Bandung, and there were also several smaller localities. These churches must have had over 500 saints. In East Malaysia, the churches in Sibu, Kuching, and Bintulu had at least 250 saints. These are very conservative numbers. Thus, we can say that twenty years ago, the churches in Southeast Asia had around 2,000 saints.

If we assume a ten percent rate of increase each year from 1965 to 1985, then in 1966 there should have been 2,200 saints, in 1967 there should have been 2,420 saints, and so on. An annual rate of increase of ten percent is equivalent to ten persons gaining one person in a year and a hundred persons gaining ten persons per year. Businessmen know that if they cannot make a profit of $1,000 with $10,000 in a year, then they should close their business. In any case, we have to present our fruit because this is a principle in the New Testament. In the Gospel of Matthew, the Lord Jesus was seeking fruit to eat (21:18-19).

Statistics are very helpful wherever they are applied. No matter what a person does, he cannot have accounting without also having statistics. Accounting is for statistics, and statistics are for the setting up of policies. The operation of our business is all based on statistics. Only when we have statistics will we know how to establish a direction in which we may proceed. If we have been in a certain business for twenty years and have not even gotten a ten percent profit, then we must close our business, change to another business, or make some personnel changes. The establishment of a business's operational direction must be decided according to accounting and statistics. Therefore, last year in Taipei we did this very thing. When we laid out the accounting and statistics, we saw that the work in Taiwan needed a change in its system. We determined that we could no longer do our work in the way we had been doing it. Not only had we failed to make a profit, but we had even lost some of our principal. Because of this, the work in every locality had no way to advance.

We can no longer go on doing something in vain, nor can we stay in self-delusion—always feeling that we are so good and so wonderful because we have the truth and life. If we would look at the statistics carefully, we would see the real situation of everything. The real situation is that the Lord has not gained much among us. If this situation persists, then even after two hundred years, the Lord's recovery still will not have a way to progress and spread. I hope that the younger generation would especially take this word and go on properly and faithfully before the Lord. There is no problem on the Lord's side for the churches in the recovery to increase and spread; the problem is on our side.

I hope that the older saints who may have several decades of experience will wake up to see that the situation is wrong and needs to be adjusted. I also hope that all the young people will see the statistics and take them as a reminder and a direction for their advance. May we all bow our heads and pray, "O Lord, forgive us; we have limited You too much, and we have failed You in too many matters. The problems are truly all on our side."

We have all seen a three-legged race. With this race, it is not a matter of how fast or how slow the contestants walk. Rather, it is a matter of whether or not they can cooperate and coordinate with each other. If one of the contestants runs very fast and the other runs very slow, then they will easily fall and be unable to rise up again. Consequently, they will remain in the same place and have no way to go forward. Today we are tied together to the Lord in a three-legged race. However, often when He walks, we do not walk, or when He does not walk, we walk. As a result, this three-legged race is not in step or in unison. Hence, how our future will be and how the church will advance both depend on how we cooperate and coordinate with the Lord. If we have much prayer, much pursuing of the truth, and much entering into the truth, we will have more knowledge and experience of the Lord. Thus, we will have more supply, the number of saved ones will naturally increase, and the power to retain them will be strong.

THE WAY TO SPEAK FOR THE LORD
OUTSIDE THE CHURCH MEETINGS

Speaking to the New Believers
Who Have Not Yet Entered the Church Life

We must have a way for the church to be able to retain the new believers. According to our past experience in Taiwan, only about five out of one hundred people who were baptized remained. In other words, out of one hundred children who were born, ninety-five died prematurely and only five remained. This kind of result is frightening. We therefore picked up the burden to study how to nourish and bring to maturity the newly saved ones after they are baptized. We all know that after a child is born, he needs to be fed. Otherwise, he will die prematurely. At this time, both in the small groups and in the church life, we are all gaining people. However, the urgent need at present is to find a way to retain and feed the newly baptized ones so that they may be perfected and may grow in life.

Based on our past experiences and present observations, we realize that besides speaking for the Lord in the meetings to supply the saints, we also have to speak for the Lord outside of the meetings to retain and perfect the new believers. The way to speak for the Lord outside of the meetings is first to speak to the new believers who have not yet entered into the church life and to render them care. We must commit the newly saved brothers and sisters to the care of specific saints. For example, if we have fifty new ones baptized, we have to commit every one of them to the definite care of a certain brother or sister. For example, if twenty of these are new brothers and thirty are new sisters, then we must properly arrange for the brothers to take care of these twenty new brothers and also for some sisters to take care of the thirty new sisters. For each new one there should be at least one brother or sister who regularly meets and takes care of that one new one. Some who are more experienced may be able to take care of two new ones. Then you should charge them, saying, "This is your child, so you have to care for him properly." In this way the responsibility will be clearly given to them.

Second, in our practice we must be flexible and not too rigid. In the past we were too rigid in our practice in Taipei. Everyone was going to meetings, especially those with some responsibility. They had meetings nearly every night of the week and morning watch every morning. Besides these meetings, there were various kinds of services. Consequently, these experienced and responsible ones did not have time to feed and take care of the new ones. All they could do was constantly exhort the new ones to attend the meetings. A newly baptized believer, however, cannot see the importance of the meetings. To illustrate, if you tell a newborn baby, "You have to eat," he will not be able to comprehend. However, this was exactly what we did in the past—we were always asking people to do something. We asked them to come and listen to the gospel; after they listened, we asked them to believe and be baptized; and after they believed and were baptized, we asked them to come to the meetings. This was very difficult for those who were asked to do all these things.

The reason why we are changing the system is that we intend to change these situations. Of course, it would be best if the newly saved ones voluntarily and regularly came to the meetings after their baptism. According to our observation, however, most of the newly saved ones are not enthusiastic about attending the meetings. They may come this week and not come the next two weeks, or they may come for two weeks and then stop coming for the next three months. If we do not contact them within half a year, it is likely that they will never come again. Now we want to change the way we do things. In the past we would go to see the new believers in person or call them on the phone and repeatedly ask them to come to the meetings. As a result, they would get disgusted and refuse to take our calls because they felt that we were trying to force them to do something. Now we need to change this. We need to accommodate them by going to their homes to meet with them, once a week if possible. Whereas in the past we asked people to come to the meeting, now we need to go and meet with them. This can be likened to "guerilla" tactics, which are more flexible and effective.

For example, suppose we have fifty people who were baptized today. Thirty of them are sisters and twenty are brothers, so we commit the thirty new sisters to the care of thirty sisters, and the twenty new brothers to twenty brothers for shepherding. At this time, we should ask these thirty sisters and twenty brothers to use the methods of "guerrilla warfare" to lead and care for the fifty new ones. This means that in caring for the new believers they should not have a set formula. Rather, this may require the shepherding saints to go and fellowship with the new ones who are being shepherded in order to find out their real condition and, based on their real needs, to make appointments with them, finding opportunities to pray and read the Bible with them. After a while, such a habit will become their natural practice, and they will appreciate every meeting.

Furthermore, we need to see that our main objective in

meeting together with the new ones should not be to exhort them to attend the meetings, to be zealous, and to serve. Rather, we should go to feed them and to minister to them. No matter what we are learning in the church meetings, whether it is something from the *Truth Lessons* or from the *Life Lessons,* we have to be like one who carries hot food from the oven to the new ones who are under our care. We have to feed them with this hot food. We do not need to read a whole lesson every time we go to them. Maybe we can read half a lesson or a quarter of a lesson. This is how to fight using "guerrilla warfare." At the initial stage we must not expect the new ones to be able to listen to so much. We must keep the principle of not forcing people. We should decide how much to feed them, depending upon their real condition and capacity. If we care for these new ones like the way a mother feeds her child, then in half a year to a year, we could have ninety who remain out of every one hundred who are newly saved.

We all have been saved and have grown in life by being under someone's care. Caring for the new believers requires us to continue steadfastly, not forcing people, pushing people, or compelling people. There is no way for new believers to go on too fast, so we need to accommodate them. Every time we go to see them, we should give them a small amount of truth, a small amount of food, and we should pray together with them. We must believe that the grace of the Lord is there. As long as we go to visit them, we can bring them a small measure of grace. In this way, in less than a year we will be able to retain people. This is the best way.

Another way to take care of the newly saved and recently baptized ones is to gather them together to practice the church life for three or five days. Every day we could speak the gospel and the truth to them, thereby giving them a start. We also need to teach them a little about certain matters they should know after being baptized, such as how to be a Christian, how to read the Bible, and how to pray. However, this kind of help is not complete. We still have to commit each of these new believers to the care of the saints. We all need to learn this matter. We should not go to people to drag them to the meetings; rather, we have to go to be with them, meeting with them in their homes.

Although the Catholic Church has many shortcomings, some of their practices are very good. For instance, if one of their members is sick in the hospital, they will send the mass to him on the sick bed. This captures people's hearts. Although there are many heresies in the Catholic Church, their practices are very flexible and tactful. Therefore, their rate of increase is very high. We are just the opposite. We are rich in truth yet somewhat rigid in our practice. This is where we need adjustment. This is also the reason for changing our system. We cannot continue to expect people to come to the meeting hall; rather, we have to go to be with them. Moreover, the Lord Jesus said, "For where there are two or three gathered into My name, there am I in their midst" (Matt. 18:20). This kind of gathering of two or three is right, and it is also what the Lord is after.

We cannot be negligent. This requires us to be equipped with the truth. Perhaps we may go and visit the saints, and all we can say is, "How are you? Thank the Lord you have been baptized. It is so good and so blessed to be baptized. Now we are all in the Lord and in the church." Following this, however, we have nothing else to say. This is not sufficient. If someone should ask us further, "How can the blood of the Lord Jesus wash away my sins?" and we remain silent, without a word and unable to answer, then he will not get any help and may even be stumbled. Hence, we all must be equipped in the truth, so that we can preach the truth to people.

Man has an inner desire to seek for knowledge, so we must try our best to satisfy the needs of the saints regarding the truth. In particular, after a person is saved, he has an inner desire to know more about the things of God. When we speak the truth and minister life to people, this brings out the desire and longing within them for the truth. Sometimes people may ask us questions that we cannot answer. We cannot tell them that we do not know the answer, and we also cannot pretend that we do know it; otherwise, people will not easily accept our words. Hence, we definitely must be equipped with the truth. If we speak the truth frequently to people and speak it clearly, we will gain their heart, and they will naturally welcome our visitations very much. Then we can gradually invite them to attend the meeting on Lord's Day. In this way they will be brought into the church meeting. Hence, in taking care of people we must not be rigid and inflexible.

I believe that this is a very sure way to retain people. Although we cannot say that we will be able to retain one hundred percent, at least we will retain seventy percent. If one hundred people are baptized, then we should keep seventy, or two-thirds, of them. Everyone who works for the Lord, even those who have been saved for many years, must practice this point. We must be confident that when new believers have passed through this kind of help and perfecting by us, gradually, after a year or so, they also will be able to help take care of others. In this way this practice will become the tradition of our family. It is impossible to depend only upon the elders to do this; every one of us must rise up and enter into the depths of the truth.

Speaking to the Unbelieving Relatives and Friends

The second way for us to speak for the Lord outside of the church meetings is to speak to a second category of people—our own unbelieving relatives and friends. We know that with relatives, there are close relatives, such as parents, grandparents, and siblings, and there are also distant relatives, such as the cousins of both of our parents. The Chinese have a saying: "Someone three thousand miles away may be a relative of ours," meaning that even a very distant person may be linked to our family. In other words, anybody could be a distant relative.

In Acts 1:8 the Lord Jesus said, "But you shall receive power when the Holy Spirit comes upon you, and you shall be My witnesses both in Jerusalem and in all Judea and Samaria and unto the uttermost part of the earth." For every one of us who is saved, our "Jerusalem" is our close relatives, our "Judea" is our distant relatives, our "Samaria" is our neighbors and colleagues, and our "uttermost part of the earth" is our friends. The gospel has to be propagated in this way unto the uttermost part of the earth.

Hence, all of us who hear this message have to make a list of all our unsaved relatives and friends, and then we need to pray for them in a faithful way and preach the gospel and the truth to them. In order to speak to them, we must definitely learn the truth. When we are learning to speak the truth to people, we also must learn to quote from the Bible and tell them about the wonderful things in the Bible. Most people oppose believing in Jesus and also oppose the Bible in a superficial way because they merely judge the Bible according to their concept without knowing its content.

About sixty years ago most of the learned Chinese despised the Bible. They despised the Chinese version of the Bible even more because it was written in the Chinese vernacular. They despised it to such an extent that they said, "What can you find in the Bible? All it contains is just *ni-men* (you), *o-men* (we), *ta-men* (they), and *ah-men* (amen). What is so profound about these things? You cannot find philosophy or science in the Bible. It is read merely by those who have little education." The foreign missionaries who came to China to preach the Word were also greatly misunderstood and opposed. When I came out to work for the Lord after I was called, I encountered similar situations. Therefore, I spent much effort to find some fundamental truths in the Bible. Then I began to speak these truths to people, and I would also open the Bible to show them where a particular truth could be found and then ask them to read the passage. The result was that they were so surprised, because they saw that the philosophy in the Bible was much higher and deeper than the philosophy of Confucius and Mencius.

In the past we had a co-worker who was a Manchurian and a member of the Kuomintang, the Chinese Nationalist Party. He was very zealous and very patriotic. At first he greatly despised Christianity. He thought that Christianity was a completely Western religion and that it was a tool used by imperialism to invade China. One day, however, as he was taking a walk, he came to a temple on a mountain. In it there

was a large-print Bible laid open on the table used for offer-
ings. He was surprised to see it, so he took it and saw that it
was opened to Psalm 1. He said in his heart, "Let me see what
Christianity is all about, and what the Bible talks about."
After reading Psalm 1, he was greatly surprised and marveled
at what was written in the Bible. He then lingered in the
temple and continued reading. That day the Holy Spirit did a
great work in him. No one preached the gospel to him, but
he was remorseful to such a great extent that he rolled on
the ground, weeping and crying. That day he was really saved
and became a Christian.

Therefore, all those who have been saved, and in particular the young people, have a responsibility to speak the truths
in the Bible to their relatives and friends. This is not merely
to persuade them to believe in God, but to clearly present to
them the treasures in the Bible. There are many testimonies
of how parents who were against their children's believing in
the Lord Jesus gradually were subdued and saved through
their children's speaking of the words of the Bible to them.
Therefore, we all have to learn to speak God's word to our
relatives and friends but not to argue with them, because the
more we argue, the more they will be annoyed and will not
listen to us. All we need to do is to present the truth to people.
Moreover, do not expect to do a quick job, thinking that once
you preach the gospel, your parents will be saved right away
just like those who were saved on the day of Pentecost. Even
if there is this kind of situation, it will not happen too frequently. We need to speak to them continually, little by little,
just like water flowing out in a trickle. This week you speak
a little, and then next week you again speak a little. In this
way, little by little over an extended period of time, your
parents will be impressed and eventually will be saved.

Although I was born into a Christian family, not all my
family members were saved. After I was saved, I loved to read
the Bible. Besides the time spent doing my homework, I
would read the Bible almost all day long. My brother, who was
four years younger than I, saw this and was very much moved,
so he also started to read the Bible and was clearly saved.
Therefore, the key to whether or not people will be saved is

whether or not we can present the biblical truths to them and show them that we are those who love the truth and read the Bible.

Instead of arguing with people, we should bring them to the Word and read the Word with them. If they are not willing to read with us, then we should read a portion to them. For example, we may read to them Romans 8:2: "For the law of the Spirit of life has freed me in Christ Jesus from the law of sin and of death." After the reading, we can point out to them that this verse speaks about two laws: one is the law of the Spirit of life and the other is the law of sin and of death. They might respond by saying, "I do not care for either law; neither do I understand such things." At this moment we should not be discouraged. Although they may say something in this way, the Lord's word has already been "injected" into them. After we leave, it is very possible that they would think, "The Bible says that the law of the Spirit of life has freed me from the law of sin and of death; this is quite marvelous." The Lord will give them the light as they recall the word.

However, maybe when we see them again, they are still acting stubborn, showing no sign that they agree with us. We should nonetheless give them another "shot" of the Lord's word, perhaps reading to them John 5:24, where the Lord Jesus said, "He who hears My word and believes Him who sent Me has eternal life, and does not come into judgment but has passed out of death into life." Most people do not like to hear such words as "judgment" and "out of death into life," but we can tell them that the Lord Jesus said that if we would believe in Him, we would have eternal life and would not come into judgment but would pass out of death into life. People may seem to refuse to listen, but at least these divine words have already entered into them. If the person hearing these words is your father, he might think, "It does not seem too bad that my child believes in such a religion. It's incredible that he can actually speak such words as 'the law of the Spirit of life,' 'the law of sin and of death,' and 'eternal life.'" Once he begins to consider in this way, he affords the Holy Spirit the opportunity to work in him.

If you go to speak to your father the third time, it is quite likely that this time he will have a turn and say, "Every time you have come home, what you have spoken to me has not been bad. It seems that this Bible has some real things in it after all." This then would open the door for him to believe. Then you have to bring out more treasure. For example, you may introduce to him the booklet titled *Three Lives and Four Laws* and ask him to read it. Do not think that it is too deep and not suitable for the preaching of the gospel. We have to see that the whole Bible is the gospel. If your father would read the booklet, the Holy Spirit would have the opportunity to take a further step in him, causing him to feel that what the Bible teaches is something wonderful which he had never heard before. He would discover that when man was created, he received the life of man; when he became fallen, he received the life of Satan; and when he was saved, he received the life of God. Furthermore, there are four laws. In addition to the law of God, every life has a law in it. When your father reads this, his heart will be softened and will change its direction. At that moment you can lead him to pray.

Do not just tell people, "Believing in Jesus is so good! Everyone is sinful, and he who does not believe in Jesus will go to hell." If we only speak such things, then people will be disgusted and will have a negative reaction; besides, these things are too low and shallow. Therefore, we have to learn the truth so that we can speak God's word outside of the meetings to the unbelievers. This depends on whether or not we have the burden and whether or not we have the heart to do it. If we have the heart, then the more we do it, the more we will have the burden. The more burden we have, the more results we will have, and the more results we have, the more we will be encouraged. To preach the gospel and bring people to salvation is not too difficult a matter. This requires us to learn the truth and to learn to speak outside of the meetings to the unbelievers.

The working saints all have many colleagues, so they have many opportunities to speak. Therefore, it is best for them to have in their pockets a small Bible, some gospel tracts, some gospel booklets, or some simple spiritual booklets, so that whenever there is a need, they can be used. We should not simply say that the Lord Jesus is wonderful, and that believing in the Lord Jesus will give people peace. Rather, we must begin with the truth. We should use the truth as the starting point and show people the truth. The truths in the Bible are the highest. No human philosophy can compare with the Bible. However, we have to learn to dig out these treasures from the Bible. Then in our daily living when there are suitable opportunities, perhaps during the noontime break or maybe after office hours, we can speak to one of our colleagues, and we can also open our Bible and read a portion to him. If he is receptive, we can give him a small booklet to read at home. We should not ask him about it the very next day; rather, we should wait for three or five days and then give him a Bible verse, again in a relaxed manner. If we work in this way persistently, people will believe in the Lord.

There is a real story which took place in Tsinan, Shantung in China. There was a brother who worked for the provincial government. He went to America to study water conservation, and after graduation he came back to China to help the province of Shantung regulate the Yellow River. At that time he had not yet believed in the Lord, but there was a believer, a brother who loved the Lord very much, who was working under him. Every morning when this brother came to clean the office, he made his manager's desk very clean and orderly and placed a gospel tract on top of the desk. When the manager came to work, he sat down at the desk and discovered the gospel tract. At first he was annoyed when he saw it, and he immediately threw it into the wastebasket. Every day it was like this, and he continued throwing the tracts away for half a year or longer. Although he threw the tracts away when he saw one, the next day the cleaning brother would place another one on his desk, and the third day he would do the same. After the manager threw away one tract, the brother would place another one; every day the brother would place a new tract. This caused the manager to become very annoyed. But after a long while, one day he suddenly thought, "This person has been doing this for such a long time, so there surely must be a reason and there must be something special here. I must speak to him to find out what this is all about." In this way the manager was saved, and subsequently his wife also was saved. In addition, both of them became very zealous for the church.

This is a good illustration for not being discouraged in the preaching of the gospel. This is also the way for us to spread and propagate. Every one of us has many people around us. The Bible tells us to be fishers of men, and the people around us are the fish. Today we do not even need to go fishing. The fish are jumping at our feet, and we can grasp them easily. Therefore, we must know the truth and speak the truth frequently to people. We have to find opportunities to preach the truth to our relatives, including our uncles, aunts, grandparents, and cousins. If we would practice this, then in a year, in 365 days, we will be able to gain at least one "fish." We will bring at least one person to salvation.

If you save one, if I save one, and if each one of us saves one, we will have an increase of one hundred percent. Not only so, if we can save one, we should be able to save two. To save one is not difficult, and to save two is even less difficult. Very often after we save one, another one follows. Sometimes after a husband is saved, the wife would follow and be saved; sometimes after a wife is saved, the husband and children would eventually follow. We have seen this matter very clearly. The problem today is that our knowledge of the truth is not sufficient and that we do not know how to introduce the truth to people. People who have been to Hong Kong know that the merchants selling precious stones there bring out their expensive jewelry to show to the customer, and when the customer's heart is touched, he naturally pays a high price to buy it. We Christians often are very foolish because we do not know how to bring out the treasures in the Bible to show to people. We have plenty of treasures at home, but we do not know how to bring them out. This is due to our lack in our daily pursuing and being equipped.

For this reason we definitely have to schedule all kinds of educational courses in the church meetings to teach the brothers and sisters so that they may be built up in the truth. Then when they go out to contact people, everyone will have his function. For a country to be strong, it must provide widespread education, and its citizens must be highly educated. In this way the country will naturally be strong. If we have education as a base, it will not be difficult to do anything. We are for the testimony of the Lord, but if we are not strong in the truth, then without that base, whatever we speak to others will be in vain. Conversely, if we have been equipped with the truth, then whatever we speak will benefit others.

Speaking to Christians in General

The third way for us to speak for the Lord outside of the meetings is to speak to Christians in general. Christians are the third category of people that we should speak to. Today although the number of Christians is not so great, neither is it that small, so we will always be able to meet some. When we meet them, we should not argue with them concerning doctrines because there will be no end to it. The best way is to set before them the truths, the precious truths in the Bible, especially those concerning Christ, so that they may be attracted.

Today in all kinds of Christian organizations, there is insufficient knowledge concerning the following four big categories of truth—Christ, the Spirit, life, and the church. The truths they know are quite superficial; however, now they also have started to treasure these four truths. Many of them have read *The Knowledge of Life* and *The Experience of Life*. Therefore, we must minister the truth to Christians to meet their need.

Avoiding Two Things

There are two things we need to avoid. First, when we are speaking with others, we should not give them the sense that we are teachers or that we are speaking with a teaching attitude. We have to be like learners, fellowshipping with them in mutuality. Second, we should not try to draw people to our meetings as soon as we contact them. There is no need for this. Wherever they want to go for meetings and however they want to meet, we should let them have their choice. Our responsibility is to release the truth and to minister life, because we are for the Lord's testimony. Whether people come

to our meeting or not, we should let them choose and not try
to draw them over. However, we must endeavor to save the
unbelievers. Our attitude is not to draw people out of Christianity into our midst. Our responsibility is to release the
truth and to minister life.

CONCLUSION

If we enter into the truth and are equipped with the truth,
and if at the same time we also receive the burden from the
Lord in prayer, then we will naturally take care of the new
believers whom we are feeding by speaking the truth to them
frequently. At the same time we will also surely have the
burden to preach the gospel to our relatives, friends, and
neighbors. Of course, we will also care for the Christians we
meet, releasing the truth to them and supplying them with
life. This is the Lord's commission to us.

Although we do not have a great number of people, if all
of us would proclaim the truth in this way, then the Lord
Jesus could have a glorious increase on the earth. Therefore,
when we meet together, we should do nothing but learn the
truth. When we go out and meet people, we should also speak
nothing but the truth. The first group of people we need to
take care of is the newly baptized ones among us. Then we
need to take care of our relatives, our friends, and other
Christians. By this we can see that our responsibility is very
great and that this work is actually without end. If we all
endeavor together with one heart, we will surely reap the
fruit. The final result will be that the church will multiply
and increase.

ABOUT THE AUTHOR

Witness Lee was born in 1905 in northern China and raised in a Christian family. At age 19 he was fully captured for Christ and immediately consecrated himself to preach the gospel for the rest of his life. Early in his service, he met Watchman Nee, a renowned preacher, teacher, and writer. Witness Lee labored together with Watchman Nee under his direction. In 1934 Watchman Nee entrusted Witness Lee with the responsibility for his publication operation, called the Shanghai Gospel Bookroom.

Prior to the Communist takeover in 1949, Witness Lee was sent by Watchman Nee and his other co-workers to Taiwan to insure that the things delivered to them by the Lord would not be lost. Watchman Nee instructed Witness Lee to continue the former's publishing operation abroad as the Taiwan Gospel Bookroom, which has been publicly recognized as the publisher of Watchman Nee's works outside China. Witness Lee's work in Taiwan manifested the Lord's abundant blessing. From a mere 350 believers, newly fled from the mainland, the churches in Taiwan grew to 20,000 in five years.

In 1962 Witness Lee felt led of the Lord to come to the United States, settling in California. During his 35 years of service in the U.S., he ministered in weekly meetings and weekend conferences, delivering several thousand spoken messages. Much of his speaking has since been published as over 400 titles. Many of these have been translated into over fourteen languages. He gave his last public conference in February 1997 at the age of 91.

He leaves behind a prolific presentation of the truth in the Bible. His major work, *Life-study of the Bible,* comprises over 25,000 pages of commentary on every book of the Bible from the perspective of the believers' enjoyment and experience of God's divine life in Christ through the Holy Spirit. Witness Lee was the chief editor of a new translation of the New Testament into Chinese called the Recovery Version and directed the translation of the same into English. The Recovery Version also appears in a number of other languages. He provided an extensive body of footnotes, outlines, and spiritual cross references. A radio broadcast of his messages can be heard on Christian radio stations in the United States. In 1965 Witness Lee founded Living Stream Ministry, a non-profit corporation, located in Anaheim, California, which officially presents his and Watchman Nee's ministry.

Witness Lee's ministry emphasizes the experience of Christ as life and the practical oneness of the believers as the Body of Christ. Stressing the importance of attending to both these matters, he led the churches under his care to grow in Christian life and function. He was unbending in his conviction that God's goal is not narrow sectarianism but the Body of Christ. In time, believers began to meet simply as the church in their localities in response to this conviction. In recent years a number of new churches have been raised up in Russia and in many eastern European countries.

OTHER BOOKS PUBLISHED BY
Living Stream Ministry

Titles by Witness Lee:

Abraham—Called by God	0-7363-0359-6
The Experience of Life	0-87083-417-7
The Knowledge of Life	0-87083-419-3
The Tree of Life	0-87083-300-6
The Economy of God	0-87083-415-0
The Divine Economy	0-87083-268-9
God's New Testament Economy	0-87083-199-2
The World Situation and God's Move	0-87083-092-9
Christ vs. Religion	0-87083-010-4
The All-inclusive Christ	0-87083-020-1
Gospel Outlines	0-87083-039-2
Character	0-87083-322-7
The Secret of Experiencing Christ	0-87083-227-1
The Life and Way for the Practice of the Church Life	0-87083-785-0
The Basic Revelation in the Holy Scriptures	0-87083-105-4
The Crucial Revelation of Life in the Scriptures	0-87083-372-3
The Spirit with Our Spirit	0-87083-798-2
Christ as the Reality	0-87083-047-3
The Central Line of the Divine Revelation	0-87083-960-8
The Full Knowledge of the Word of God	0-87083-289-1
Watchman Nee—A Seer of the Divine Revelation ...	0-87083-625-0

Titles by Watchman Nee:

How to Study the Bible	0-7363-0407-X
God's Overcomers	0-7363-0433-9
The New Covenant	0-7363-0088-0
The Spiritual Man 3 volumes	0-7363-0269-7
Authority and Submission	0-7363-0185-2
The Overcoming Life	1-57593-817-0
The Glorious Church	0-87083-745-1
The Prayer Ministry of the Church	0-87083-860-1
The Breaking of the Outer Man and the Release ...	1-57593-955-X
The Mystery of Christ	1-57593-954-1
The God of Abraham, Isaac, and Jacob	0-87083-932-2
The Song of Songs	0-87083-872-5
The Gospel of God 2 volumes	1-57593-953-3
The Normal Christian Church Life	0-87083-027-9
The Character of the Lord's Worker	1-57593-322-5
The Normal Christian Faith	0-87083-748-6
Watchman Nee's Testimony	0-87083-051-1

Available at
Christian bookstores, or contact Living Stream Ministry
2431 W. La Palma Ave. • Anaheim, CA 92801
1-800-549-5164 • www.livingstream.com